Carpathia

Food from the Heart of Romania

IRINA GEORGESCU

Interlink Books

An imprint of Interlink Publishing Group, Inc.
Northampton, Massachusetts

Contents

Introduction

Romania is a culinary melting pot. Its character is rooted in many cultures from Greek, Turkish, and Slavic in the south and east, to Austrian, Hungarian, and Saxon in the north and west. In *Carpathia* I aim to introduce you to this authentic, bold, and delicious cuisine and in doing so, take you on a culinary journey to the very heart of this fascinating Eastern European country, exploring its history, landscape, and traditions through food.

The Carpathian Mountains are an imposing presence in Romania's landscape, and I couldn't have chosen a better namesake for a book that speaks about a country of fairy tale forests, misty peaks, rolling hills, lush green pastures, and the ancient shores of the Black Sea.

There is a lot to say about Romania's cuisine, but there are very few voices that have told the stories. In these times, when tolerance and inclusion seem to be losing ground, I hope that a book about Romanian cooking will help to dispel some of the misconceptions about Romania and its people. I can't think of a more delicious way to get to know us than by enjoying our food, and I hope that you will agree with me.

Food is intertwined with personal journeys and life stories. It can create a bridge that connects us across borders, languages, and cultural differences. When I cook the recipes in this book—making *borş*, grilling peppers, crushing garlic for *mujdei*, making pickles—the fragrances remind me of how Romanian cooking is part of the collective European heritage and landscape. This is why some of the dishes look familiar, or their names speak of a German, Hungarian, or Turkish origin. A friend said to me about some of the recipes, "you can't put them in, they are not Romanian!" but what is traditional Romanian cooking if not the amalgamation of influences that we've made our own?

I want this book to be an acknowledgment and celebration of Romanian home cooking, our culinary heritage, and who we are as people. I have kept as close as possible to the traditional ingredients and flavors, how my mom used to cook, but also bringing the recipes together in my own way. To me, and to many like me living away from our homeland, food is a way of remembering our roots and bringing back memories. To us food brings comfort and the sweet feeling of belonging, wherever and whoever we are.

A Romanian childhood

I grew up in Bucharest under communist rule. The city was crowded with apartment blocks where the central heating was on for only 4 hours a day. The working week was Monday to Saturday, and television was restricted to 2 hours a day. We would stand in lines for rationed food for two or three days in a row, and sometimes go home empty-handed. The limited availability of food heavily influenced the dishes we were able to cook at home, so we improvised. If we couldn't get the right ingredients to make cakes or desserts, we would eat compotes and jams instead.

Our apartment was only 430 square feet (40 square meters) and was home to our family of four together with my dad's mother Maria, who lived with us from November to March each year. My mom's parents, mamaie Domnica and tataie Gheorghe, also lived in Bucharest, having met there in their youth, one coming from Transylvania, the other from the south, in Oltenia. This was a fiery combination!

My dad, Constantin, a metallurgical engineer with patented inventions, was very ambitious. To him, doing your best wasn't good enough. My mom, Lucia, was an elementary school teacher who changed careers and worked in IT for the army. She was also a wizard in the kitchen. Every day after work my mom would look after the house, cook delicious food from incredibly scarce ingredients, and help with our homework. This is what women were expected to do in those days, and it wasn't easy. My mother was the one who held us all together.

It is from my parents' work ethic and my mom's culinary ingenuity that I draw my values in life. When I started to follow my culinary dreams I learned a lot about my new country of residence, the UK, through its food and met some incredible people. I hope that, in the same way, you will learn a lot about Romania through the recipes in this book, my family stories, and the history of our staple ingredients.

The heart of Romanian cuisine

Romanians are fun-loving people. We like to eat well, surrounded by family and friends, and welcome guests. The food we cook is not complicated, but it reflects the communality of how we eat. Appetizers are often served mezze-style with plenty of sharing plates, and main dishes sometimes require a little patience, allowing more time to enjoy the company of family and friends. Our mothers are our culinary bibles, passing down recipes from their grandmothers to us, so it's no wonder that cooking is very personal to us. Read on for a tour of our staple ingredients.

Porc (pork): We love pork in bold, deeply-flavored dishes. Rich and incredibly addictive, you can't resist a second helping. As with all types of meat, we cook with the cheap cuts and offal to make the most of this resource. Nothing goes to waste. Pork is very often the star of our summer barbecues, with its wonderful succulence and gorgeous aroma.

Mămăligă (coarse polenta): Ubiquitous in our cooking, throughout this book you will find polenta in the ingredients lists for appetizers, main courses, side dishes, and even desserts. It's the perfect carrier for an abundance of flavors and ingredients.

Borş (broth): This traditional Romanian ingredient will surprise you. Chapter three is dedicated to it, featuring a multitude of delicious, tangy recipes that can be made with it.

Mere (apples): This beloved fruit is used in both savory and sweet dishes, and surprisingly in pickles, too. In a country blessed with the right climate for growing fruit trees, apples play a big part in many dishes. Fruit with meat and a sweet-sour combination of flavors speaks very much of the Persian influence, probably influenced by the Macedonian Greeks who settled in Romania.

Usturoi (garlic): Almighty in our cooking, from *Mujdei* (see page 209)—a garlic vinaigrette—to fine slices of raw garlic added to a stew right at the last minute, garlic is ever present in our cuisine. Said to be a powerful protector against evil spirits and able to predict a marriage, garlic dishes may be spicy and strong, mellow and sweet, or nutty and delicate, much like the Romanian temperament.

Brânză (cheese): Telemea is reminiscent of halloumi and kasseri, firm and set in brine. Caşcaval and brânză de burduf are similar to the Italian caccicavallo, hard creamy alpine cheeses. Urdă and brânză de vaci are tangy, set-curd cheeses, similar to ricotta, and usually the only cheeses that are made at home. They are essential fillings in Romanian pies and desserts, often mixed with herbs or enriched with eggs and raisins and then flavored with vanilla and citrus rind.

Iaurt (yogurt), *lapte covăsit* (thick-set yogurt), and *smântână* (sour cream): These dairy products are widely used in recipes for pastries and doughs. In Romanian food shops, the yogurt counters are filled with tubs of yogurt and sour creams from different parts of the country. The vendor will ladle out the required quantity for you and off you go.

Murături (pickles): We adore pickles, especially whole cabbages fermented sauerkraut-style with green tomatoes, called *gogonele* (see page 186). The mild acidity of these brined pickles cuts through rich dishes without the need for a fruit sauce or relish. Our pantries reflect the multitude of flavors that we pack into our pickles: lovage, parsley, winter savory, dill, thyme, cinnamon, caraway seeds, vanilla, walnuts, and raisins.

Vin (wine): Romanian wine is recovering at a steady pace from a dark time when vineyards were collectivized, native grapes lost, and craftsmanship forgotten. Wine is made in every part of the country. At Cotnari in Moldova, we make a golden-yellow wine with notes of apricots and walnuts called *Grasă de Cotnari*. In Dobrogea, between the Black Sea and the Danube, we have the Murfatlar vineyards, with its Chardonnay, Muscat, and Pinot Gris grape varieties. In the south, we have the famous Domeniile Tohani vineyards, founded in 1773, enjoying the same climatic conditions as Bordeaux and producing the famous velvety red *Fetească Neagră*, from a Romanian grape variety with the same name. The rosé (and also a wonderful red) comes from Banat, in the south-west, from Cramele Recaş. Last but not least, famous and ever present on our tables, the *Jidvei* dry wines of Transylvania in the Târnave Valley, a region first mentioned for its vineyards by the Greek historian Herodotus in 5th century BC.

CHAPTER ONE

Food is for sharing: small plates, appetizers, and salads

At a Romanian table, you will be served our beloved mezze-style appetizers. Platters of charcuterie—the famous *Pleşcoi* sausages and *Sibiu* salami—are served accompanied by pickles, cheese, and cured pork fatback called *slănină*.

You will taste the Romanian version of eggplant caviar and charred pepper salad, hummus-style lima beans with caramelized onions, fish salads and *icre* (carp's roe taramasalata). Try a sheep's milk cheese with a juicy slice of ripe tomato and fresh pickled cucumber, or a piece of lardo on potato bread with red onion.

We begin the feast on the right note by passing shots of *ţuică* around. Be careful though, this plum brandy is strong stuff.

It is no secret that we love polenta in Romania. You will find some intriguing recipes here, which hopefully will encourage you to eat polenta more often and enjoy its versatility and delicious, corny flavor.

Vegetables love our climate and we grow some amazing tomatoes, green beans, and peppers bursting with color and flavor. Crunchy, prickly cucumbers, scallions, and garlic are part of any vegetable garden, and it is so rewarding to grow your own zucchini. The highlight of our summers are the giant watermelons—so sweet they almost crystallize in the middle. Then autumn descends upon us with its silky ribbed-skin pumpkins and aromatic apples.

In cities, where we can't have gardens, we go to markets, which are full of fantastic produce. When the harvests are at their peak, these markets overflow onto neighboring streets, and it is a joy to be able to buy fresh produce every day instead of doing one big weekly shopping trip in a standard supermarket.

Mămăligă cu brânză si smântână

Cheesy polenta with sour cream and runny
fried egg—a full Romanian breakfast

This *mămăligă* is a satisfying, comforting breakfast. Easy and cheap
to make, it offers a sunny start to the day whatever the weather.
There is a certain type of cheese that goes with this dish called
brânză de burduf, a spicy, crumbly cheese that is often matured
in pine bark cases, not easy to get a hold of outside of Romania.
An alternative would be a spicy blue cheese such as Gorgonzola
however, a good mature Cheddar will also do the trick.

Serves 4

1¼ cups (300 ml) milk

⅔ cup (150 ml) water

1 cup (5 oz/150 g) coarse polenta

4 tablespoons (2 oz/60 g) butter

1½ cups (6 oz/175 g) crumbled
    blue cheese or grated Cheddar,
    plus extra to serve

¼ cup (60 ml) sour cream

4 fried eggs

Salt and freshly ground black pepper

Bring the milk and water to a boil in a pan over low heat. Turn the
heat to medium and stir in the polenta. Keep stirring for about
10 minutes, adding more hot water if necessary, until the mixture
reaches the consistency of thick porridge and slowly falls off the
spoon. Add the butter and cheese and mix well until melted and silky.
Season with salt and pepper and divide between pasta bowls. Top
each portion with a dollop of sour cream and a fried egg. Sprinkle
with more cheese and black pepper to serve.

Ardei copți

Charred pepper salad with garlic vinaigrette

Here are the flavors of Romanian summers: sweet charred peppers, bathed in tangy garlic sauce. The trick is to choose perfectly ripened peppers, so that the flesh won't stick to the skin when it's peeled off.

Heat a griddle pan (or grill) to high heat and char the peppers evenly on all sides, turning often, until they become soft. Peel the skins away very carefully, keeping the stalks attached. Combine the vinegar with a pinch of salt, then add the oil and garlic. Stir to emulsify, then taste. If it's too vinegary, add a splash of water or another pinch of salt. Arrange the peppers in a star shape, stalks up, in a shallow bowl, then gently pour over the vinaigrette. Leave the flavors to infuse for at least 30 minutes before serving.

Serves 4–6

4–6 bell or Romano
    peppers
1 tablespoon apple
    cider vinegar
Salt
3 tablespoons olive oil
1 garlic clove, very
    finely chopped,
    almost to a paste

Salată de vinete

Eggplant caviar with red onion and fennel seeds

Romanians love eggplants, and when I was a child every August we would each try to be the first to eat the new eggplants of the season. My mom would have a special deal with her favorite vendor to keep some aside until she came back from work in the late afternoon, otherwise the eggplants would have been sold or used to bribe the local officials.

Serves 4–6

Char the eggplants as the peppers above. Sprinkle the salt over the skins and put them to drain on a tilted chopping board, so any juices can run off. While the eggplants are still warm, cut them in half lengthwise and scoop out the flesh. Roughly chop the flesh and put into a non-metallic bowl.

Add the oil to the bowl little by little, stirring with a wooden spoon after each addition. Add the onion, vinegar, and a little salt, combine, and taste for seasoning. Sprinkle with fennel seeds—they are my favorite, but not quite traditional.

Spread on good crusty bread and eat with the charred pepper salad (above), or use as a filling for juicy summer tomatoes for a cheerful lunch.

4 firm, ripe eggplants
1 teaspoon salt
¼ cup (60 ml) olive oil
1 medium red onion,
    finely diced
1 tablespoon balsamic
    vinegar
1 teaspoon dried
    fennel seeds
Crusty bread, to serve

Zacuscă

Makes 2 lb 4 oz (1 kg)

4 eggplants

4 bell peppers

3 medium onions, peeled

2 carrots, peeled

1 celeriac (celery
   root), peeled

⅓ cup (80 ml) olive
   oil or canola oil

2 cups (500 ml) tomato
   passata or purée

Scant ½ cup (3½ oz/
   100 g) tomato paste

7–8 bay leaves

Hot paprika

Salt and freshly ground
   black pepper

Equipment:

4 x clean half-pint (8 oz/
   225 g) jars

Charred autumn vegetable dip

In Russia, *zacuski* are bite-sized appetizers served as an accompaniment to vodka, but in Romania this refers to a charred vegetable dip. This dip is frequently eaten at Lent, bringing a bit of color to the gloomy days of restriction.

Preheat the oven to 325°F (160°C). Char the eggplants and peppers (see page 19), then set aside to cool. Scoop out the eggplant flesh and peel the peppers, discarding the stalks and seeds. Using a food processor, pulse the eggplant flesh and peeled peppers together, then transfer to a bowl. Next, pulse the peeled vegetables. Heat ¼ cup (60 ml) of the oil in a heavy ovenproof pan over medium heat and sauté the pulsed vegetables for 25 minutes, adding a splash of water to avoid burning. When almost caramelized add the eggplant and pepper mixture, the remaining 4 teaspoons oil, and the remaining ingredients. Season with paprika, salt, and pepper. Transfer the uncovered pan to the oven and cook for 1¼ hours, stirring every 30 minutes, until the mixture is reduced to the consistency of a dip. Transfer to the clean jars and cover. Store in the refrigerator.

Fasole bătută

Serves 4–6

For the lima bean dip:

3 garlic cloves

2 x 14 oz (400 g) cans
   lima beans, drained

6 tablespoons olive oil

1 teaspoon salt

6 tablespoons water

For the caramelized
onions:

Vegetable oil or sunflower
   oil, for frying

2 white onions,
   finely sliced

1 teaspoon sweet paprika

1 teaspoon sugar

Scant ½ cup (100 ml)
   tomato passata
   or purée

Romanian lima bean dip with sweet caramelized onions

This is a gorgeous, garlicky dip that is very popular throughout the year and often served the night before St. Andrew's Day. It's believed that the garlic keeps evil away and spiritually cleanses the house. Serve on thick slices of bread topped with the addictive caramelized onions.

To make the dip, pulse the garlic briefly in a food processor, then add the lima beans. Gradually add the oil, combining well, until fully incorporated. Set the food processor to the lowest speed and add the salt and water, mixing well for a few seconds. Set aside.

   To make the caramelized onions, cover the bottom of a frying pan with a thin layer of oil and turn the heat to high. When it's hot, add the onions and stir to ensure they are well coated in oil. Add a splash of water to avoid burning. Reduce the heat to medium and cook for around 10 minutes, stirring from time to time, until soft and golden. Add the paprika, sugar, and passata. Cook until everything melts into a deep orange color, stirring frequently. Remove from the heat and leave to cool. Serve the dip in a bowl topped with the caramelized onions.

Slănină

Romanian pork lardo

Diced thinly and eaten raw with bread and red onion, *slănina* is the most famous of all Romanian charcuterie. Tourists always see it as a curiosity: "Do you really eat raw pork fat?" they ask, eyes wide open in perplexity. Usually prepared and cold-smoked in the countryside, this recipe is more like an "apartment version" of the whole process, but it's a good starting point with fabulous results.

Mix the salt, pepper, and garlic together in a bowl. Massage this dry rub all over the fatback, then place it in a plastic container. Put the lid on and refrigerate for 3 months.

Remove the fatback from the fridge. Rinse with cold water, pat dry using a dish towel, and leave uncovered in the fridge overnight. Some people like to roll it in paprika at this stage, which will create a rich, dark-red outer layer.

Serve sliced on toast or add to dishes to enrich their flavor. I keep mine wrapped in parchment paper in the freezer, and only cut a slice when I need it.

Makes 1 lb 2 oz (500 g)

½ cup (6 oz/175 g) salt

¼ cup (1 oz/30 g) black pepper

6 garlic cloves, minced

1 lb 2 oz (500 g) pork fatback, rind-on (or 2 x 9 oz/250 g stacked)

Sweet paprika, for rolling (optional)

Urzici cu usturoi

Stinging nettle fricassée with garlic flakes and pumpkin seeds

This dish is the first thing we eat in spring and is the pinnacle of cooking local, seasonal, and fresh. We buy the nettles from the market and bag them in huge quantities, trying to carry them home without getting stung. They are very much like spinach: you think you are going to feed a whole village with them, but once in the pan they reduce to a few spoonfuls. Nettles are the superfoods of March and April, full of vitamins, especially vitamin C and iron. We don't throw away the blanching water, but drink it as a fortifying tea, making the most of this wonder-plant. Its flavor is very green, invigorating, quite earthy, and slightly sweet.

Pick nettles when they first appear in March and the plants are still young. Wear gloves and gather the top 6 to 8 leaves of each spear. You can substitute spinach, but the flavor will be different.

Serves 4

12 oz (350 g) stinging nettles

1 tablespoon olive oil, plus
    extra for drizzling

1 small white onion, finely chopped

14 garlic cloves, peeled

1 tablespoon all-purpose flour

2 tablespoons coarse polenta

4–5 scallions, green tops only

Salt

½ cup (2 oz/60 g) roasted
    pumpkin seeds, to serve

Grated Cheddar cheese, to serve

Fill the sink with cold water. Wearing rubber gloves, place the nettles into the water, ensuring they are totally submerged. Pick the leaves, removing the thicker stalks, and transfer to a dish.

Fill a large bowl with cold water. Bring 6 cups (1.5 liters) of water to a boil in a large pan, add the nettles (in batches, if necessary), and blanch for 5 minutes. Transfer the nettles from the pan to the bowl with cold water. Reserve 2½ cups (600 ml) of the cooking water.

Heat the oil in a frying pan over high heat and sauté the onion until soft and translucent. Slice 7 of the garlic cloves and add to the pan. Continue to cook for 2 minutes, then add the flour and polenta. Cook for a few more minutes, stirring well. Add the cooking water from the nettles a little at a time, then add the drained nettles.

Reduce the heat to medium and cook for 8 minutes, stirring occasionally. Finely slice the remaining garlic cloves and add to the frying pan, along with the scallions and a generous pinch of salt. Combine well, while cooking for a further 2 minutes. It may look like a large quantity of garlic, but it will be totally absorbed by the nettles.

Taste, and adjust the seasoning if necessary. Serve warm, garnished with pumpkin seeds, a drizzle of olive oil, and a sprinkle of grated cheese. Accompany with bread, fried eggs, or cooked polenta.

Bulz

Oven-baked cheese polenta balls served with yogurt and roasted tomatoes

Polenta can't get any more original than this. In Transylvania, where my mom comes from, *bulz* is made in the oven, but in the south it is flattened and griddled like a patty. Being a shepherd's meal, the polenta balls are often thrown into the embers of an open fire, especially when dinners are enjoyed in the cool air of summer evenings. I dare you to try this next time you are having a barbecue—you can wrap the balls in aluminum foil, if you wish.

Bring 2 cups (500 ml) of water to a boil in a large pan over high heat. Add the polenta, butter, and salt, whisking quickly to avoid any lumps forming. Turn the heat down to medium and keep whisking for 5 minutes until the polenta thickens considerably. Add the Cheddar cheese and yogurt, mix briefly, then spread the hot polenta onto a baking sheet. Leave to cool for around 20 minutes.

Preheat the oven to 400°F (200°C). Using wet hands, take ⅓ cup (2 oz/60 g) of polenta and flatten it in your palm. Add a little sheep or goat cheese in the middle and close your hand, rolling the polenta into a ball—you will get confident after the first one—and place onto a baking sheet. Repeat with the remaining polenta then bake for 25–30 minutes until the balls are golden and crisp on the outside.

Meanwhile, place the cherry tomatoes onto a third baking sheet, drizzle with oil, and roast for 15–20 minutes.

Serve the *bulz* straight from the oven with the roasted cherry tomatoes and a dollop of yogurt.

Serves 6

1½ cups (9 oz/250 g) coarse polenta
2 tablespoons (1 oz/30 g) butter
1 teaspoon salt
3½ oz (100 g) Cheddar cheese, grated
1 cup (9 oz/250 g) plain yogurt
5 oz (150 g) hard sheep or
    goat cheese, grated
1½ cups (9 oz/250 g) cherry tomatoes
Olive oil, for roasting

To serve:
Scant ½ cup (3½ oz/100 g) plain yogurt

Salată de peşte

Smoked mackerel salad with tarragon and mayo

This is one of the first dishes I ever made on my own. My mom trusted me with it completely, mainly because it was an assembling job rather than actual cooking. But I took it as a compliment. Mayo is time-consuming to whisk by hand, so she was more than happy to park me in the kitchen with something useful to do. The tarragon is my own "adult" addition—its subtle anise flavor goes so well with fish.

Serves 2

For the mayo:

1 cup (250 ml) sunflower oil

1 tablespoon rapeseed oil

2 egg yolks

Juice of 1 lemon

1 teaspoon Dijon mustard

Salt and freshly ground black pepper

For the mackerel salad:

9 oz (250 g) smoked mackerel

1 large onion (half finely diced or
    grated; half finely sliced)

3 pickled cucumbers, diced and drained

1 bunch of tarragon, chopped

To make the mayo, combine the oils in a jug. Place the egg yolks into a bowl and add the oil a little at a time, whisking continuously and incorporating each addition fully before adding more oil. Do this with an electric whisk or by hand, if you like a good challenge! Once all the oil has been added, the mixture should have formed a smooth, shiny, thick mayo. Add the lemon juice and mustard, season with salt and pepper, and stir to combine. Refrigerate until ready to use.

To make the mackerel salad, remove the skin from the mackerel, carefully shred the flesh, and place into a large bowl. Mix in all the onion and pickled cucumbers, making sure they are evenly distributed. Add just enough mayo to bind everything together then sprinkle over the tarragon. Serve with more mayo on the side.

Dovlecei pané

Zucchini fritters with garlic sauce

Zucchini are used widely in Romanian cuisine. We make fritters, patties, stews, *borș*, stuff them, grill them—you name it. One year my dad decided to turn a patch of land that my grandmother used for growing corn into a vegetable garden. This was the beginning of a new hobby. He used to drive for a couple of hours every day after work so that he could water the vegetables in the evening when the scorching heat of the sun could no longer harm them. My sister and I insisted on planting zucchini , since we loved the fritters. That year we even made zucchini jam! That's how staggering the harvest was.

Serves 4–6

Slice the zucchini into ½ inch- (1 cm-) thick discs and pat dry using a dish towel. Combine the flour and polenta (if using) in a shallow dish. Place the egg in a separate dish. Heat the oil in a frying pan over high heat. Working in small batches, dip the zucchini slices in the flour, then in the egg. Carefully place in the oil and fry for 2 minutes on each side, then set aside on paper towels to drain any excess oil. Repeat with the remaining slices, fitting as many as you can into the pan at once. Season the fritters with salt and pepper and serve on a plate with a generous drizzle of garlic sauce and a sprinkle of parsley—perfect for a lunch-time snack.

4 zucchini
Generous ¾ cup (3½ oz/100 g)
    all-purpose flour
1 tablespoon coarse polenta (optional)
1 egg, beaten
¼ cup (60 ml) vegetable oil
    or sunflower oil
Salt and freshly ground black pepper
Garlic sauce (see page 209), for drizzling
½ bunch of parsley, chopped, to serve

Caşcaval pané

Breaded alpine cheese

Caşcaval is a buttery, pale yellow semi-hard cheese with delicious sweet undertones. It is made of cow or sheep's milk, and is often cold-smoked. Its mild flavor and melting qualities make it the perfect ingredient in many traditional dishes. Served as part of an appetizer platter, the taste and texture are similar to the Italian caciocavallo and Greek kasseri. The method for making it is called *pasta filata*, which means "stretched curd."

    Caşcaval is difficult to find outside Romania, so I'm using the all-time favorite Cheddar here because it can achieve the perfect balance between melting and barely holding its shape together.

Serves 2

7 oz (200 g) block of Cheddar cheese
⅔ cup (2½ oz/75 g) all-purpose flour
1 egg, beaten
½ cup (2 oz/60 g) breadcrumbs
Vegetable oil or sunflower oil, for frying

Cut the block of cheese in half horizontally to make two thinner rectangles. (If you find it difficult to slice, cut the block into smaller rectangles, similar to fish sticks.) Place the flour, egg, and breadcrumbs into three separate shallow dishes. Heat a little oil in a frying pan over high heat. Dip each cheese rectangle in the flour first, followed by the egg and then breadcrumbs. Fry for 2 minutes on each side. Serve with a fried egg or sliced tomatoes for a rich and delicious breakfast for all the cheese lovers out there.

Alivenci

Moldovan polenta cakes with cheese and dill

These cakes are often served to mark important occasions: birthdays, celebrations, expressions of love, the arrival of guests, and farewells. To me, they are the spirit of Moldova, perhaps only matched in fame by the Byzantine painted monasteries of Sucevița and Voroneț. Moldova is culturally rich in terms of traditions, folklore, and culinary ingenuity, as these cakes prove with their unexpected, silky elegance.

Bring the milk to a boil in a pan over medium heat, then add the butter and polenta. Stir continuously for a few minutes until thickened, then set aside to cool slightly.

Meanwhile, separate the eggs and place the yolks and whites into separate bowls. Mix the yolks with the ricotta, feta, yogurt, flour, and dill, then add this mixture to the lukewarm polenta along with the baking powder. Stir to combine well.

Preheat the oven to 400°F (200°C) and grease a 11 by 9 inch (28 by 23 cm) baking pan. Whisk the egg whites until they form stiff peaks. Carefully fold the egg whites into the polenta mixture. Pour into the pan and bake for 40 minutes, or until a skewer comes out clean. Do not remove the polenta from the oven—turn it off and don't open the door for 20 minutes.

Turn the polenta out onto a chopping board, slice, and serve warm with sour cream and more dill, as an appetizer or lunch.

Serves 8

2¼ cups (500 ml) whole milk

4 tablespoons (2 oz/60 g) butter

1¼ cup (7 oz/200 g) coarse polenta

4 eggs

1¼ cups (10½ oz/300 g) fresh
    ricotta (see page 210)

7 oz (200 g) feta, crumbled

1 cup (9 oz/250 g) plain yogurt

½ cup (2 oz/60 g) all-purpose flour

1 bunch of dill, finely chopped,
    plus extra to serve

1 teaspoon baking powder

Sour cream, to serve

Tort de clătite cu spanac

Goat cheese and spinach crêpe cake

Serves 6–8

For the crêpes:
Generous 1½ cups (7 oz/200 g)
      all-purpose flour
2 eggs
2¼ cups (550 ml) whole milk
Salt
Vegetable oil or sunflower
      oil, for frying
Butter, for crêpes

For the filling:
2 tablespoons (1 oz/30 g) butter
1 onion, finely diced
1 lb (450 g) spinach, wilted,
      squeezed of water, and
      shredded in a food processor
1 bunch of dill, finely chopped
9 oz (250 g) goat cheese
2 eggs
1 tablespoon plain yogurt
4 scallions, finely sliced
Nutmeg
Salt and freshly ground
      black pepper

For layering:
5 oz (150 g) ball mozzarella, grated

For the egg mixture:
1 egg, beaten, mixed with
      1 tablespoon plain yogurt

This is a real show stopper at dinner parties, with its delicate crêpes filled with goat cheese mousse and buttery spinach. We used to make it at springtime, when spinach was in season and sold in tall loose bunches, similar to chard, at the market. You can make the crêpes and the filling a day ahead, then bake just before serving. Take your time and enjoy the process—it is not difficult and pretty foolproof.

To make the crêpes, combine the flour, eggs, milk, and a pinch of salt in a bowl and refrigerate for 1 hour. Heat a tablespoon of oil in an 8 inch (20 cm) frying pan. Add enough batter to thinly and evenly coat the base of the pan, tilting the pan to move the mixture around. Leave to cook for about 30 seconds until golden underneath, then ease a spatula under the crêpe to lift and flip it over. Add a pat of butter each time you flip. Cook for a further 30 seconds, then transfer to a plate to cool. Repeat with the remaining batter. You will need 12 crêpes.

To make the filling, heat the butter in a pan over medium heat and sauté the onion. Add the shredded spinach and stir briefly while some of the water evaporates. Take the pan off the heat, add the chopped dill, and set aside to cool. Combine the cheese with the eggs, yogurt, cold spinach mixture, scallions, and a pinch of nutmeg. Season well with salt and pepper. The mixture should just fall off the spoon. Cover and set aside.

Preheat the oven to 350°F (180°C). To assemble the cake, I prefer to use a shallow baking dish slightly larger than the crêpes but you could also use a baking sheet. Place 1 crêpe in the bottom of the dish, spread ¼ cup (2 oz/60 g) of the filling on top, sprinkle with a little mozzarella, then top with another crêpe. Repeat the layering until you run out of filling, finishing with a crêpe on top. Brush the top with the egg mixture and sprinkle with any leftover mozzarella.

Bake for about 30 minutes, covering the top with aluminum foil halfway through if it looks too caramelized. Serve barely warm or even cold. The crêpe cake will keep in the fridge for a couple of days.

Salată de castraveți

Cucumber and red onion salad

A totally refreshing, thirst-quenching salad that is perfect for hot summer days. In Romania, *castraveți* are cucumbers with a slightly bitter taste and thick, prickly skin. In my family, we would eat them straight from the vine while gathering the harvest and deciding what to do with them. Some were ideal for making summer pickles in brine, left to mature outside in the sun for 2–3 days in earthenware jars. We would put these pickled cucumbers in the fridge and drink the brine instead of water. Other cucumbers would make it into a salad such as this one, accompanying steak or fish dishes.

Slice the cucumber into thin rounds. Cut the onion in half and slice it finely, then quickly run it under cold water to remove its pungency and let the subtle flavors come through. Pat the onion dry. Combine the onion and the cucumber in a small bowl, distributing the onion evenly. Mix in the salt, tarragon, vinegar, and oil, coating the cucumbers well. Serve immediately before the cucumbers lose their crunch. This makes for a refreshing side dish, or add some white crumbly cheese and a slice of bread for a good lunch.

Serves 2–4

1 large cucumber
½ red onion
1 teaspoon salt
¼ bunch of tarragon,
    finely chopped
2 tablespoons apple
    cider vinegar
1 tablespoon olive oil or
    rapeseed oil

Salată de varză

Shredded white cabbage salad

This is the ultimate crunchy salad. It is tangy, peppery, and I usually slice the white tender core of the cabbage very thinly and add it to the salad, too. It's delicious and tastes like kohlrabi. On days when I don't eat meat, I add walnuts and raisins for a light lunch.

In a large bowl, mix the cabbage with the salt and set aside for 15 minutes—the salt will extract moisture from the cabbage and soften it. When ready, squeeze the cabbage well before transferring to another bowl. Add the remaining ingredients, season with pepper, and serve immediately.

Serves 2–4

½ small white cabbage,
    finely shredded
2 teaspoons salt
¼ bunch of dill, finely
    chopped
1 tablespoon olive oil
1 lemon, cut into wedges
Freshly ground
    black pepper

Salată de sfeclă cu hrean

Beet and horseradish salad

I am very fond of beet salad with freshly grated horseradish root, whether on its own or as an accompaniment to broths or stews. It is light, vibrant, and easy to prepare. It is especially popular in the winter and up until April, in part due to the belief that if we eat horseradish before Easter, we'll be healthy all year round.

Serves 4

4 beets
Sunflower or vegetable oil, for baking
¼ horseradish root
1 tablespoon white wine vinegar
2 tablespoons olive oil
1 teaspoon honey
Salt and freshly ground black pepper
1 bunch of fresh fennel or dill, roughly
    chopped (optional), to serve

Preheat the oven to 400°F (200°C). Wash the beets well, then rub each one all over with a little oil and wrap in aluminum foil. Bake for 30–35 minutes, then set aside to cool. Meanwhile, finely grate the horseradish root. Combine the vinegar and oil with the horseradish then add the honey and season with salt and pepper to taste. Grate the cooked beet, place everything in a salad bowl, and garnish with fresh fennel or dill, if desired. The salad can be stored in a jar for a few days before serving. Match it with Smoked Ham Hock and Lima Bean Casserole (see page 99).

Salată de vară

A summer medley salad

Serves 4

Tomatoes thrive in the hot Romanian summers. They become large, fleshy, juicy, and sweet, and can be eaten like apples. Paired with onions and Romanian telemea cheese, they make for a perfect picnic snack to be enjoyed at the side of the road on long drives. This salad is more of a restaurant lunch version, a celebration of all our summer flavors.

Mix all the ingredients, except the boiled eggs, together and set aside for 5 minutes to allow the flavors to infuse. Transfer to a serving dish and add the eggs, if desired.

3 medium tomatoes, sliced or quartered

½ large cucumber, finely sliced

1 small head Boston or romaine lettuce, shredded

3 scallions, sliced

½ cup (3½ oz/100 g) pitted black olives

3½ oz (100 g) Romanian telemea cheese or feta, crumbled

2 tablespoons olive oil

1 teaspoon balsamic vinegar

2 hard-boiled eggs, peeled and halved (optional)

Salată de fasole verde

Green and yellow French beans with onion vinaigrette

I like to eat this salad as often as I can, while the beans are still young and tender. To test for freshness, snap the beans in the middle. If there is a thin thread keeping the halves together, you need to buy from another vendor, since this one is trying to sell you old beans!

Serves 2

For the vinaigrette:
¼ white onion, finely diced
2 garlic cloves, finely sliced
1 tablespoon apple cider vinegar
¼ cup (60 ml) olive oil

For the salad:
14 oz (400 g) green and yellow
    French beans, trimmed
Salt and freshly ground black pepper
1 oz (30 g) feta cheese, to serve (optional)
Slivered almonds, to serve (optional)

To make the vinaigrette, combine the onion with the garlic and vinegar. Pour in the oil, stirring well to combine. Leave to infuse while the beans are cooking.

Put the beans in a large pan and cover with water. Bring to a boil over high heat, then add 1 teaspoon of salt. Turn the heat to low and cook for 15 minutes or until just tender but still with a crunch. Have a bowl of ice-water on hand and quickly transfer the beans to the bowl to stop them from overcooking. Set aside to cool for 3 minutes.

Season the salad with salt and pepper and serve drizzled with the vinaigrette. Enjoy for lunch topped with feta cheese and slivered almonds (if you like), with or without bread.

CHAPTER TWO

Breads and
street-food bakes

Bread is the staff of life and Romanians treasure it greatly, making it a part of everyday life—from street food to celebrations and traditions. We love a white bloomer called *franzelă*, or a crescent brioche roll called *corn*, but we also happily eat flatbreads, or *scovergi*, which we sometimes stuff with meat, sauerkraut, potatoes, cheese, or fruit. These flatbreads or pastries take on so many different names—*plăcintă*, *şuberec*, *merdenea*, *brânzoaică*, or *învârtită*. We dip the pretzel-like *covrig* in yogurt for a lunch on the go, or buy a little bag of *sărățele* to nibble while we do our shopping.

Colac is a round bread loaded with symbolism. Plain or heavily decorated with braids and flowers, the loaves may be small or weighing up to 9 lb (4 kg). *Colac* is traditionally served at weddings, funerals, baptisms, harvest, and religious celebrations. It is made for *Dragobete*—our Valentine's Day—or for St. Andrew's Night—our Halloween—and offered to carol singers at Christmas alongside walnuts and apples. The round shape signifies infinity and the rhythm of the seasons, while the wheat grain represents the giving of life and renewal.

Official guests, including presidents and royal families, are welcomed with bread and salt; the bread to celebrate an alliance, the salt for prosperity.

Scovergi

Yogurt and cheese flatbreads or "Romanian popcorn"

When I was growing up, these cheesy, gooey flatbreads were something to munch on while chatting around the table, or watching television in the living room, even when television was on for only 2 hours a day and full of programs about the achievements of the Communist party. There wasn't any popcorn or snacks in those days, so we passed the *scovergi* around the room instead.

Mix the flour, yogurt, yeast, egg, salt, and water together in a large bowl. Knead briefly until well incorporated, then cover and refrigerate for 2 hours. It will be a fairly sticky dough, but will become more friendly after resting.

Flour a work surface and knead the dough well, then stretch it to a ⅛ inch- (3 mm-) thick circle. Sprinkle a little flour on top of the dough if it is too sticky. Sprinkle the cheese evenly all over the dough, then roll it up to make a log approximately 16–18 inches (40–45 cm) long. Cut the log into 8 equal pieces.

Take one piece of dough and place it onto the work surface cut-side up, so you can see the layers. With a rolling pin, roll it out into a 7 inch (18 cm) circle. Heat 1 tablespoon of the oil in a large frying pan over medium heat. Fry the flatbread for 3 minutes on each side, or until it turns a beautiful golden color. Repeat with the remaining dough.

Place the flatbreads on a plate and cover to ensure they stay moist and gooey and do not become dry and crisp.

Makes 8 x 7 inch (18 cm) flatbreads

4 cups (1 lb 2 oz/500 g) all-purpose
    flour, plus extra for flouring
1 cup (9 oz/250 g) plain yogurt
2 teaspoons (¼ oz/7 g) active dry yeast
1 egg
1 teaspoon salt
1 tablespoon water
7 oz (200 g) Cheddar cheese, grated
½ cup vegetable oil or sunflower oil

Pită cu cartofi

Potato bread in cabbage leaves

My great-aunt Fira had a wood-fired oven in a small room next to the main house. This was typical of Transylvanian villages, where people would use outbuildings for daily household tasks. The village women would bake bread there and every two weeks, it was somebody else's turn to host the others. Their traditional method for *pită* was to wrap it in cabbage leaves, which formed a natural steamy environment—essential for a flavorful crust. I was so obsessed with Fira's homemade *pită* that come December, she would send me one big, fat wheel of bread as an early birthday gift.

To make the *maia,* prepare it the evening before baking. Mix all the ingredients together in a large bowl until well combined. Cover and leave in a warm place overnight.

The following day, after around 12 hours, add the dough ingredients to the *maia.* Transfer to the bowl of an electric mixer fitted with a dough hook and knead for 15 minutes on medium speed. Cover and leave to rise for 1½ hours or until doubled in size.

Meanwhile, line an 8 inch (20 cm) round cake pan with the cabbage leaves in a single layer, making sure they overhang the edge of the pan by about 1 inch (2.5 cm).

When the dough is ready, flour a work surface and your hands. Turn the dough out onto the work surface and gently knead and fold it a few times. The dough will be fairly wet and you'll need to work quickly. Form a ball by bringing your palms underneath the dough, rotating a few times. This whole stage should take only 1–2 minutes. Place in the cabbage-lined pan, cover, and leave to proof for 40–45 minutes.

Preheat the oven to 425°F (220°C). Carefully bring the overlapping cabbage leaves to the middle of the proofed dough—they don't have to cover the dough entirely—and bake for 40 minutes. The cabbage may burn but that's okay.

Carefully remove the bread from the pan and return it to the oven, upside-down, for a further 10 minutes. Leave to cool, then scrape away the cabbage, slice the bread, and serve with butter.

Makes 1 loaf

For the *maia* (pre-ferment):
½ cup (2 oz/60 g) white bread flour
1 cup (9 oz/250 g) mashed potatoes
Scant 1 cup (200 ml) water
½ teaspoon (¹/₁₆ oz/2 g) active dry yeast

For the dough:
4 cups (1 lb 2 oz/500 g) white bread flour, plus extra for flouring
⅓ cup (80 ml) water
2 teaspoons salt
½ tablespoon (⅛ oz/5 g) active dry yeast

For baking:
Leaves of 1 Savoy cabbage

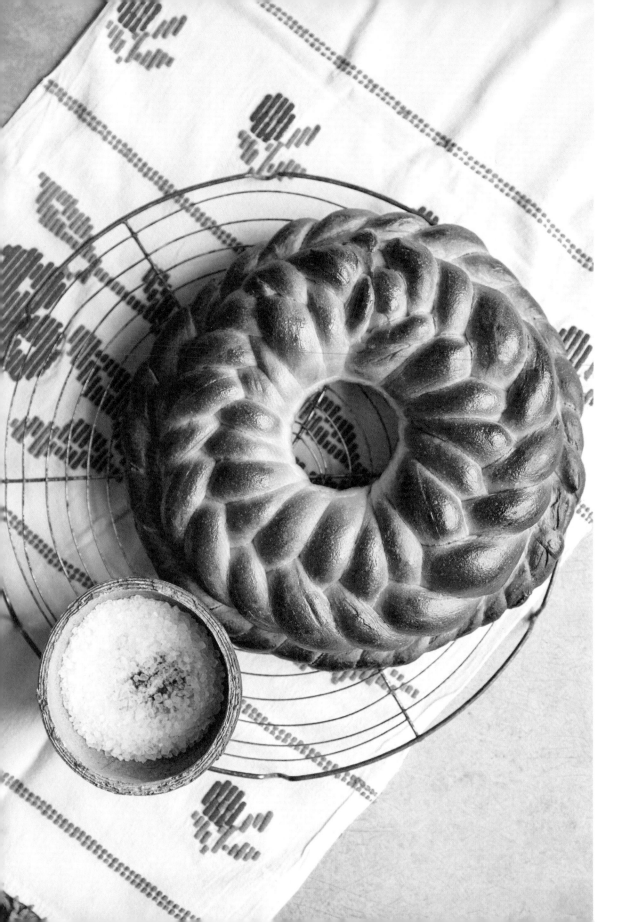

Colac

Braided bread

Romania is the land of wheat, and these round breads are eaten daily. The recipes vary from plain, as this one here, to enriched doughs with many eggs and lots of butter—it depends on the occasion. Folk wisdom says that if we stick some of the raw dough to fruit trees in spring, they will have a bountiful year. This bread is also torn over the bride's head at weddings in the hope that the crumbs will predict the number of children she will have.

Combine all the ingredients in the bowl of an electric mixer fitted with a dough hook. Knead for 8–10 minutes (or by hand for 15 minutes). Cover and leave to rise for 1½ hours in a warm place.

Turn the dough onto a work surface—there is no need to flour it. Divide the dough into 6 balls. Roll 5 into 20-inch (50-cm) long strands, then unite all 5 at one end, keeping the loose ends closest to you. Lightly flour each strand.

To make the braid, take the first strand on the left-hand-side and bring it across to the middle between the four remaining dough-strands. Now take the fifth strand on the right-hand-side and bring it across to the middle between the four remaining strands. Repeat, always taking the outside strand across to the middle between the other four. Work fairly tightly to achieve an even pattern, but not too tight, as you need to allow the dough room to expand.

Trim the top end where you first united all the strands. Bring both ends together, uniting them in a ring, leaving a hole in the middle (if you have a small baking ring or round cookie cutter, place it in the middle, but it's not necessary).

Take the sixth ball, divide in two, and roll into 24-inch (60-cm) long strips. Overlap the two strips in the middle in an X shape. Twist together the top half of the X, then do the same to the bottom half. Lift the twisted strand and encircle the base of your bread. Cover and leave to prove in a warm place for 40 minutes.

Preheat the oven to 425°F (220°C). Brush the bread lightly with the egg mixture and bake for 40–50 minutes, covering with aluminum foil halfway through the cooking time if the top becomes too dark. Serve with butter and salt.

Serves 6–8

4 cups (1 lb 2 oz/500 g) bread flour,
    plus extra for flouring

2 teaspoons salt

2 teaspoons (¼ oz/7 g) active dry yeast

1 cup (250 ml) lukewarm water

⅓ cup (80 ml) olive oil

For glaze:

1 egg, beaten, with a dash of milk

Mămăligă

Romanian cornbread

Making cornbread was my dad's task every Sunday. We had our own corn field and the cornflour was ground at the local mill in my grandmother's village. Golden-yellow and coarse, it made a firm bread that really tasted of corn. Dad would add the polenta little by little, simmering it low and slow, then quickly turning it over onto a wooden board in the middle of the table. Traditionally, we would slice it using a cotton string and eat it in place of wheat bread.

There are a few superstitions related to this cornbread: if the top cracks, it means that you'll take a long journey. If you want to mend a broken heart, drink water from the pot where you cooked it, and think of nothing but the meal in front of you.

Serves 6–8

2 cups (500 ml) water
1 cup (5 oz/150 g) coarse polenta
1 teaspoon salt
1 tablespoon (½ oz/15 g) butter

Bring the water to a boil in a pan over high heat. Reduce the heat to low, sprinkle in the polenta, salt, and butter, and whisk continuously for 10 minutes. Simmer gently for a further 10 minutes, whisking often so it doesn't catch on the bottom. Remove from the heat and wait for 2 minutes, then quickly turn it out onto a chopping board or a plate (if it doesn't turn out easily, gently loosen it around the edges with a spatula). Then, with wet hands, shape the polenta into a dome. Leave it to cool and set before slicing.

Covrigi

Little breads with poppy seeds and salt

Covrigi have the texture of a bagel and the shape of a pretzel. They are usually eaten warm, only because no one has the patience to wait for them to cool. *A* street food staple in Romania—sprinkled with poppy seeds, sesame seeds, or left plain, they are perfect with a cup of coffee or a glass of yogurt. When you see lines in front of little bakeries on the streets of Bucharest, you'd better get in line, too, to buy one of the most delectable, crispy, warm snacks this city has to offer.

To make the dough, mix the ingredients together until the dough comes away from the sides of the bowl. Cover with a damp dish towel and leave to rise for 1½ hours in a warm place.

Oil your palms lightly and turn the dough out onto a work surface. Divide into 8 balls ready for shaping. (*Covrigi* can be shaped in two ways—below is the method for both, but you can keep it simple and choose just one.)

Shaping method one: To make a pretzel shape, roll one dough ball into to a 16–18 inch (40–45 cm) rope. Take both ends and form a loop then cross the ends over each other and bring them to the center of the loop. Place the ends in the middle of the curve of the loop, overlapping the dough.

Shaping method two: To make the intertwined ring, take one ball and divide it in two. Roll each half into 16–18 inch (40–45 cm) long strands, then cross them in the middle to form an X. Twist together the top half of the X, then do the same to the bottom half. Bring the ends together in a circle, overlapping them slightly.

Preheat the oven to 400°F (200°C) and line 2 baking sheets with parchment paper. Place four breads on each, cover with a damp dish towel, and leave to rise for 30 minutes. Brush gently with the egg mixture and sprinkle over the poppy seeds and salt.

Bake for 18 minutes. Serve warm with yogurt.

Makes 8

For the dough:

4 cups (1 lb 2 oz/500 g) white bread flour

2 teaspoons salt

1 teaspoon sugar

2 teaspoons (¼ oz/7 g) active dry yeast

Scant 1 cup (200 ml) lukewarm water

2 tablespoons (1 oz/30 g) butter, melted

1 egg

For the glaze:

1 egg, beaten with a dash of milk

3 tablespoons (1 oz/30 g) poppy seeds

Flaky sea salt

Plăcintă cu carne

Meat and mushroom pie

The story of *plăcintă* begins with the Greeks and the Romans and ends with an incredible variety of slices on Romanian tables. There, between two layers of satisfying pastry, you can have your favorite fillings—meat, vegetable, cheese, or fruit. The pastry can be made only from flour and water, or with added yeast and enriched with butter, eggs, or sour cream. In my family, we serve this version as a snack, picked-up straight from the baking sheet and eaten holding a hand under the chin to collect any escaping morsels.

To make the dough, mix all of the ingredients together in a bowl and knead for a few minutes until smooth. Cover and set in a warm place for 1 hour.

To make the filling, cover the bottom of a frying pan with a thin layer of oil and cook the onions over medium heat for 5–8 minutes. Add the ground beef and cook until browned, then add the mushrooms, passata, and paprika. Simmer until the mixture is reduced and thickened. Set aside to cool, then add the eggs and parsley, and season with salt and pepper. Stir well to combine.

Preheat the oven to 400°F (200°C) and line an 11 by 9 inch (28 by 23 cm) baking sheet with parchment paper. Lightly flour a work surface and divide the dough in two. Roll out both halves to roughly the same shape as the baking sheet—you don't have to be precise. Place one dough sheet onto the baking sheet and stretch using your fingers to cover the base and sides.

Spoon the filling onto the dough, distributing it evenly. Place the second dough sheet on top of the filling, ensuring that it covers the filling by gently stretching it with your fingers. Brush the top of the dough generously with the egg glaze.

Bake for 30 minutes, then leave to cool on a wire rack before turning out onto a chopping board. Trim the edges, then slice into long, wide strips. Each slice can be cut into three rectangular pieces, if desired.

Serves 8–10

For the dough:
2½ cups (10½ oz/300 g) all-purpose flour
⅔ cup (150 ml) lukewarm milk
3½ tablespoons (1¾ oz/ 50 g) butter, melted
1 medium egg
2 teaspoons (¼ oz/7 g) instant yeast
1 teaspoon salt

For the filling:
Vegetable oil or sunflower oil, for frying
2 onions, sliced
2 lb 4 oz (1 kg) ground beef
12 oz (350 g) mushrooms, roughly sliced
Scant 1 cup (200 ml) tomato passata or purée
2 teaspoons sweet paprika
2 large eggs, beaten
1 bunch of parsley, finely chopped
Salt and freshly ground black pepper

For the glaze:
1 egg, beaten with 1 tablespoon plain yogurt

Sărățele—"Salties"

Caraway breadsticks and loops

I've always associated these "salties" with having guests for dinner—it was my job to cut them into ribbons or make the loops when my mom was preparing them. *Sărățele* are often served when first sitting down at the table and are offered with a shot of *țuică*—the famous Romanian plum brandy. They are also our favorite food-on-the-go to be enjoyed as a snack between errands, when there is no time for lunch. You can buy them from bakeries or mini-markets across Romania, and they should really come with a warning saying, "incredibly addictive."

Serves 8–10

For the dough:

10 tablespoons (5 oz/150 g) butter, diced

2½ cups (10½ oz/300 g) all-purpose
    flour, plus extra for dusting

¼ cup (2 oz/60 g) plain yogurt

3½ oz (100 g) Cheddar cheese,
    finely grated

1 egg, beaten

1 teaspoon salt

For the topping:

1 egg, beaten with a dash of milk

¼ cup (2 oz/60 g) caraway seeds

Coarse salt

To make the dough, rub the butter into the flour until the mixture resembles breadcrumbs. Add the yogurt, cheese, egg, and salt and knead for 2–3 minutes until the dough comes together. Cover and let rest in the fridge for 30 minutes.

Preheat the oven to 350°F (180°C) and line 2 baking sheets with parchment paper. Divide the dough in two. Flour a work surface and roll one-half to a 12 by 10 inch (30 by 25 cm) rectangle, dusting the dough as you roll if it becomes too soft. Cut this rectangular in half lengthwise, then cut each smaller rectangle into 1¼ inch- (3 cm-) wide strips crosswise.

Divide the other half into tablespoon-sized balls (about ½ oz/ 15 g). Flour your hands lightly to prevent the dough from sticking, and roll each ball into a rope, 12–14 inches (30–35 cm) long. Bring the ends of each dough rope together in a loop, crossing the ends at the top to form an X.

Place both the stick and loop salties onto the baking sheets and brush very lightly with the beaten egg mixture and sprinkle generously with caraway seeds and coarse salt.

Bake for 25 minutes, or until dark golden in color. Pour a shot of plum brandy or open a bottle of beer, and enjoy as many as you wish.

Plăcintă cu cireşe de peste Prut

"Across the Prut" pie stuffed with cherries

The river Prut creates a natural border between Moldova in north-east
Romania and the Republic of Moldova, the independent state that was once
part of Romania, then Russia. Romanian is the official language in both Moldovas,
and our love for pies and stuffed breads unites us across the river. This version of
the dough has butter between the layers and can be baked rather than fried.
My mom called it *foi de plăcintă*, or "pie sheets," and used it in pies and pastries.

To make the dough, mix the flour with the egg, water, and salt. Knead for 10
minutes, then cover and refrigerate for 1 hour. Gently beat the butter with a
sprinkling of flour to form a spreadable blend. Set aside in a warm place but don't
allow to melt.

Flour a work surface and roll the dough into a 16 by 14 inch (40 by 35 cm)
rectangle, with the long side parallel to you. Spread 7 tablespoons (3½ oz/100 g) of
the butter mixture onto two-thirds of the dough rectangle from left to right—the
right third of the dough will be left bare. Fold the right side two thirds across the
rectangle, then fold the left side over to overlap it. Bring the bottom half to the
middle, and the top half to completely overlap the bottom half. It needs to look like a
closed book. Now turn its spine to your left. You may need to keep flouring the work
surface and the dough to prevent everything from sticking.

Roll again, this time to a slightly smaller rectangle than before and repeat the
process above, using 5 tablespoons (2½ oz/75 g) of the butter mixture. Roll again and
repeat the steps using the remaining butter (you need to roll the dough out three
times in total). Wrap in plastic wrap and refrigerate for at least 1 hour or ideally
overnight. The dough can also be chilled in the fridge for 30 minutes before the last
folding.

To make the filling, place the cherries, sugar, and 2 tablespoons of water in a
deep pan and bring to a boil over medium heat. Reduce the heat and simmer for
10 minutes or until thickened. Set aside to cool.

Preheat the oven to 400°F (200°C) and line 4 baking sheets with parchment
paper. To assemble, divide the pastry in four and roll one piece into a 9 inch (23 cm)
circle. Spread a quarter of the cherry mixture evenly on top, then bring the edges
of the pastry to meet in the middle, overlapping and pressing down to seal—don't
worry if the folds are not identical. Repeat with the remaining pastry.

Place the four pies on baking sheets, glaze with the egg mixture, and bake for
25 minutes. Leave the pies to cool a little, then cut into slices along the folds.

**Makes 4 x 6 inch
(16 cm) pies**

For the dough:
3 cups (12 oz/350 g) white
    bread flour, plus
    extra for flouring
1 egg, beaten
½ cup (120 ml) water
1 teaspoon salt
2¼ sticks (9 oz/250 g)
    butter, softened
    but not melted

For the filling:
1 cup (5 oz/150 g)
    pitted cherries
⅓ cup (2½ oz/75 g) sugar

For glazing:
1 egg, beaten with 1
    tablespoon milk

Kurtos kalacs

Hungarian chimney cakes

My dad used to work in Transylvania and was away for weeks at a time, spending just a few days back at home. Every time he returned he brought back food—essential for our family, as food was mostly found on the black market. We would look through his bags for something special. Sometimes there were *covrigi* (see page 58), bagels, jars of sweet chestnut purée, or—to our cheers of joy—*kurtos kalacs*, with their nutty, buttery aroma enveloping the whole of the apartment.

To make the dough, briefly whisk the eggs, sugar, and butter together. Sift in the flour and add the milk and yeast. Knead the dough for 8–10 minutes until smooth, then cover and set aside to rise in a warm place for 1 hour.

To prepare the baking molds, wrap each emptied can in a sheet of aluminum foil. Twist the excess foil at one end to create a handle, then brush the foil with melted butter.

Divide the dough into 6 balls and roll each into a ¼ inch- (5 mm-) thick rectangle. Cut into 1½ inch- (4 cm-) wide strips. Carefully wrap the strips of dough around a prepared can in a spiral, slightly overlapping them as you go. You will most certainly need to stick strips together in order to go all the way down the length of the can. Repeat with the remaining dough strips and cans.

Preheat the oven to 400°F (200°C) and line a baking sheet with parchment paper.

To make the coating, combine the sugar, walnuts, and vanilla extract in a shallow dish. Brush the dough-spirals with half of the melted butter, then roll in the sugar and walnut mixture. Arrange on the baking sheet and bake for 10 minutes. Carefully remove from the oven and brush with the remaining butter, and again roll in the sugar and walnut mixture. Bake for a further 10 minutes, or until golden brown.

Leave to cool on a wire rack for 5 minutes, then gently push the spirals off the cans. Serve warm with a large cup of coffee.

Makes 6

For the dough:

3 eggs

⅓ cup (2 oz/50 g) light brown sugar

6 tablespoons (3 oz/80 g) butter, melted

3¾ cups (1 lb 5 oz/600 g) all-purpose flour

Scant 1 cup (200 ml) lukewarm milk

1½ tablespoons (½ oz/15 g) instant yeast

For the coating:

1 cup (5 oz/150 g) light brown sugar

1 cup (3½ oz/100 g) walnuts,
    finely chopped

1 teaspoon vanilla extract

7 tablespoons (3½ oz/100 g)
    butter, melted

For baking:

6 x 16 oz (470 ml) tall beer or
    soft-drink cans, emptied

CHAPTER THREE

Borş and ciorbă

In Romania, we eat *borş* or *ciorbă* between the starter and the main course. These broths have a tangy, sour element added to them, from fermented wheat—in which case they are called a *borş*—or from vinegar, unripe summer fruits, and even brine from pickles, in which case they are called *ciorbă*. Lima beans, rice, and potatoes are used to thicken the broths, and we like to enrich them with a beaten egg mixed with sour cream after removing the pot from the heat. There are infinite variations: pork with tarragon, meatballs with lovage, lettuce with sliced omelet, sauerkraut with paprika, vegetable medley, sorrel, and even nettles. Pretty much any broth can be made into a refreshing *borş* or *ciorbă*.

Borș

The ingredient

Borș is a big thing in Romania. This juice—made by fermenting wheat bran on its own or together with polenta—is used in meat or vegetable broths to add a sweet-and-sour flavor. Thus, any broth with this flavoring is called *borș*, but it's not the beet soup that you would expect in other Eastern European countries. A true *borș* (the ingredient) is not very sour, has just the right hint of sweetness, and is pale green in color with golden reflections. Needless to say, its health benefits are right up there with kombucha, kimchi, and miso, especially if you drink one glass every morning on an empty stomach. It's the secret to a good complexion.

Makes 8½ cups (2 liters)

3 cups (7 oz/200 g) wheat bran
⅔ cup (3½ oz/100 g) coarse polenta
11 cups (2.7 liters) tepid water
1 slice of toast, almost burned
2–3 bay leaves
1 celery stick, roughly chopped
1 bunch of parsley
Few lovage stalks (optional)

Equipment:
1 x 3-quart (3-liter) sterilized jar
    with tightly fitting lid

Day 1: Combine 1 cup (2 oz/60 g) of the bran with ½ cup (2 oz/60 g) of the polenta and scant 1 cup (200 ml) of the tepid water in the jar. Seal the jar and leave in a warm place (over 65°F/18°C) for 12 hours.

Day 2: Add the remaining ingredients, seal the jar, and place in a bowl to collect any leakage. Leave in a warm place for up to a week. Open the jar every day and stir well with a wooden spoon.

After 4 days taste the *borș* before stirring—it will probably smell of fermentation. Repeat this every day after that, and once it tastes sweet-sour, then it's ready. Pour through a fine sieve into a lidded bottle or jar (or several), and place in the fridge. It is now ready to use.

The fermented bran that settles on the bottom of the jar can be used to start another batch or make a face mask—wonderful for glorious, supple skin.

Borş de fasole cu cârnaţi afumaţi

Lima bean *borş* with smoked farmhouse sausage and red onion salsa

You will find this *borş* everywhere in Romania, but to me it is especially connected to the Carpathian mountains, where winters start in September and end in May, and the food needs to give people strength. It is a delicious introduction to Romania's most loved flavors: meaty, smoky, tangy, and sharp.

Place the pork bones or ribs, peppercorns, and halved onion in a deep pot and cover with water. Bring to a boil over high heat, then quickly turn the heat to low, cover, and simmer for about an hour, skimming off any foam that forms on the surface with a slotted spoon.

While the stock is bubbling away, fry the sausages in oil for 5 minutes, and leave to cool. Once cool, cut into 1 inch (2.5 cm) pieces and set aside.

Blend together in a food processor or grate the peeled onion, carrot, and celery. Add to the stock along with the herbs, reserving a little of the parsley for garnishing. Simmer for another 1½ hours, or longer if you have things to do.

To make the red onion salsa, run the onion slices under cold water to remove their pungency and let the subtle flavors come through. Pat dry using a dish towel. Add the vinegar, a pinch of sugar, and a generous pinch of salt. Mix well and set aside to allow the flavors to infuse.

Remove the bones from the stock and discard. Carefully strain the stock, then return it to the pot and place over high heat. Add the red pepper, tomatoes, lima beans, and cooked sausage pieces. Add the *borş* or meat stock and vinegar and cook for a further 15 minutes. Taste for seasoning, adding salt and pepper if desired. Serve topped with the red onion salsa and garnished with the reserved parsley.

Serves 4–6

For the stock:

2 lb 4 oz (1 kg) meaty pork bones or ribs
10 black peppercorns
2 onions; 1 unpeeled and halved, 1 peeled,
4 good-quality sausages, hot
    smoked (see page 208)
Vegetable oil or sunflower oil, for frying
1 carrot, peeled
3 celery sticks
1 bunch of parsley
1 bunch of thyme
1 red pepper, diced
1 x 14 oz (400 g) can chopped tomatoes
2 x 14 oz (400 g) cans lima beans, drained
Scant 1 cup (200 ml) *borş* (see page 70)
    or use meat stock combined with
    ¼ cup (60 ml) white wine vinegar
Salt and freshly ground black pepper

For the red onion salsa:

1 red onion, finely sliced
1 tablespoon vinegar
Sugar
Salt

Ciorbă de salată

Lettuce broth

This is a refreshing *ciorbă*, perfect for lunch on summer days, especially when served cold. In different regions of the country and depending on the season, people use different leaves from stinging nettles, sorrel, and red mountain spinach, to wild garlic and even dandelion leaves. The sliced omelet gives it a little more body, making it a satisfying meal.

Serves 4–6

2 tablespoons vegetable oil
    or sunflower oil
1 onion, peeled and grated
1 carrot, peeled and grated
6 cups (1.5 liters) vegetable stock
2 eggs, lightly beaten
Generous ¾ cup (7 oz/200 g) Greek
    yogurt
2 heads romaine lettuce, roughly shredded
¼ cup (60 ml) white wine vinegar
3 scallions, roughly chopped
1 bunch of dill, roughly chopped
Salt and freshly ground black pepper
Olive oil, for drizzling

Heat 1 tablespoon of oil in a deep pan and cook the onion and carrot over medium heat until caramelized. Add the stock and simmer for 10 minutes.

Meanwhile, make an omelet by heating 1 tablespoon of oil in a frying pan. Slip the beaten eggs into the pan and cook for a minute on each side. Season with salt and pepper and set aside to cool. When cool enough to handle, slice into long strips.

Place the yogurt in a bowl. Add the shredded lettuce and vinegar to the broth and bring to a boil, then remove from the heat immediately. Carefully transfer some of the hot broth to the bowl with the yogurt, little by little, until the mixture is hot. Now pour it back into the pan and stir gently but well. Adjust the seasoning and add the scallions, dill, and sliced omelet. Drizzle with a little olive oil, if desired.

Serve warm or cold, though it doesn't reheat well.

Ciorbă de dovlecei umpluţi

Stuffed zucchini *ciorbă* with sour cream

With this *ciorbă*, we cross the Carpathian Mountains and stop to eat in Oltenia, in the south-west. Here lies the story of a rebellious spirit, of our famous *haiduc* Jianul—our own Robin Hood, a wealthy mid-ranking *boier*, or aristocrat, who fought for freedom from the Ottoman and Habsburg rule. It is a land of fertile plains and plump, sun-kissed vegetables cooked in the most ingenious ways. This *ciorbă* is a good example of breaking the rules and crossing the lines between a rich broth and a stew.

To make the filling, heat the oil in a frying pan over medium heat and cook the onion with the rice until the onion is soft and golden. Add the beef and cook for a further 10 minutes or until browned, stirring often. Set aside to cool, then combine with the remaining ingredients and season with salt and pepper.

To make the *ciorbă*, cut the zucchini in half or in thirds (depending on their size) and gently scoop out the seeds and a bit of the flesh to create hollow tubes. Stuff the meat filling into the hollows tightly, then set aside.

Bring the stock to a boil in a large pan over high heat. Add the tomato paste and stuffed zucchini , turn the heat down to medium, and simmer for 15 minutes, or until the zucchini are cooked but still firm on the outside and retaining their green color. Remove the pan from the heat and stir in the vinegar. Serve immediately with dollops of sour cream and mint leaves.

Serves 6

For the filling:

1 tablespoon vegetable oil or sunflower oil

1 small onion, finely diced

3 tablespoons arborio rice

7 oz (200 g) ground beef

2 garlic cloves, crushed almost to a paste

1 egg, beaten

2 teaspoons sweet paprika

¼ bunch of mint, finely chopped

Salt and freshly ground black pepper

For the *ciorbă*:

4 zucchini

6 cups (1.5 liters) homemade beef stock

Scant ½ cup (3½ oz/100 g) tomato paste

3 tablespoons white wine vinegar

To serve:

3 tablespoons sour cream

Mint leaves

Ciorbă de peşte

Fish broth with rice and sour cream

Who would have thought that there was such a thing as a fish *ciorbă*? It's a regional dish coming straight from the waters of the Danube Delta—literally! Locals use the river water to make the broth, and this is what makes it so special. It is traditional in southern Romania to serve the fish in a separate dish, followed by the broth. Chopped scallions or a salad are never far away. There are two ways of preparing this fish broth: with tomatoes and potatoes, to which we add *borş*; or with rice, to which we add sour cream mixed with egg yolk (as in the recipe below). Herbs such as lovage, dill, or fennel are added according to taste.

Bring the stock to a boil in a large pan over high heat. Add the fish and shrimp and simmer for 5–8 minutes. Using a slotted spoon, remove the fish and shrimp from the stock and set aside to cool.

Bring the stock back to a boil, add the rice, reduce the heat, cover, and simmer for 10 minutes, or until the rice is tender. Taste and adjust the seasoning by adding salt and pepper, if needed.

Combine the egg yolks and sour cream in a large bowl. Carefully transfer some of the hot broth to the bowl with the eggs, little by little, whisking continuously, until the mixture is hot. Now pour it back into the pan and stir well. Add the fennel and scallions at the last minute, to keep their flavor intact.

I like to serve the seafood and broth separately, spooning out just a little of the broth with rice from the pan to accompany the fish, but you can definitely eat them together, adjusting the quantity of the broth to your liking.

Serves 4

4 cups (1 liter) fish stock
1 lb 5 oz (600 g) cod or other firm
    white fish, cut into chunks
5 oz (150 g) shrimp
⅓ cup (2 oz/60 g) long-grain rice
2 egg yolks
1 tablespoon sour cream
½ bunch of fennel, chopped
2–3 scallions, chopped
Salt and freshly ground black pepper

Borş de perişoare

Meatballs *borş* with lovage

Serves 4–6

For the broth:

2 lb 4 oz (1 kg) beef bones

1 onion, peeled and grated

1 parsnip, peeled and grated

¼ celeriac, peeled and grated

4 bay leaves

4 juniper berries

6–7 black peppercorns

1 bunch of parsley, chopped

Scant ½ cup (100 ml) tomato
    passata or purée

Scant 1 cup (200 ml) *borş* (see page
    70) or sauerkraut juice

2 teaspoons salt

For the meatballs:

¼ cup (1½ oz/40 g) arborio rice

9 oz (250 g) ground pork

1 small onion, finely diced

1 egg, beaten

Small slice of white bread, soaked
    in milk and squeezed

½ bunch of parsley, finely chopped

2 teaspoons sweet paprika

Salt and freshly ground black pepper

To serve:

Plenty of fresh lovage or parsley

Sour cream

As I'm writing these lines, I realize how much I am longing for those moments that I can't bring back. This *borş* means home-coming to me. When we returned from a long journey, or a week spent away from home, or we had a tough time at work or an exam at school, my mom used to make us the food we loved. It was her way to be there for us, showing us love and support. This dish—comforting, rich, and welcoming—still says, "everything is going to be OK," to me.

To make the broth, put the bones, grated vegetables, bay leaves, juniper berries, peppercorns, and parsley into a deep pan and cover with water. Bring to a boil over high heat, then reduce the heat, cover, and simmer for 1½ hours, skimming off any foam that forms on the surface with a slotted spoon. (If you don't have time to make the broth from scratch, use a good-quality beef stock from your butcher.)

Meanwhile, make the meatballs. Cook the rice in a pan of simmering water for 8 minutes. Drain and add to a large bowl along with the remaining ingredients. Combine well and refrigerate for around 30 minutes.

With wet hands, roll the meat mixture into golf ball-sized (1–1½ oz/30–40 g) balls. Place on a tray, cover, and return to the fridge until you are ready to cook.

Remove the bones from the broth and add the passata, *borş*, and salt. Simmer for a further 5 minutes. Place the meatballs into the broth, reduce the heat to low, and cook for 20 minutes.

Serve immediately, with a generous sprinkle of chopped lovage or parsley and a bowl of sour cream on the side.

Ciorbă de varză acră

Caraway sauerkraut *ciorbă* with potatoes

In early spring, if there was any fermented cabbage leftover from the winter batch, we would make this *ciorbă* using both the cabbage leaves and the brine. This is a pure Saxon dish from Transylvania, specific to the region where my mom grew up, Țara Moților. Traditionally we add smoked pancetta but I prefer it without, making this a light vegan dish. The caraway seeds and smoky paprika really bring out the natural sweetness of the cabbage. You can use store-bought sauerkraut, or make your own using the recipe on page 186.

Heat the oil in a pan over medium heat and cook the onion and potatoes until softened, then add the stock and simmer for 10 minutes. Add the sauerkraut and cook for a further 10 minutes, or until the potatoes are tender.

Remove from the heat, add the paprika and caraway seeds, and season with pepper. Taste, and if you'd like a bit more tang add the vinegar. Serve sprinkled with a little more paprika or pepper and garnished with fresh thyme, if desired.

Serves 4–6

1 tablespoon vegetable oil or sunflower oil

1 onion, finely diced

2 medium potatoes, diced

6 cups (1.5 liters) vegetable stock

1¼ cups (10½ oz/300 g) shredded sauerkraut (store-bought or see page 186), drained

1 teaspoon sweet paprika, plus extra to serve

1 tablespoon caraway seeds, lightly crushed

1 tablespoon apple cider vinegar (optional)

Fresh thyme, to serve (optional)

Freshly ground black pepper

Ciorbă de porc cu tarhon

Tarragon pork rib broth with smoked pancetta

This broth is a celebration of smoky flavors balanced by the bitter-sweet taste of tarragon and the tangy yogurt.

Serves 4–6

1 lb 2 oz (500 g) pork ribs

6 cups (1.5 liters) cold water

3 bay leaves

2 onions, peeled

1 parsnip, peeled

¼ celeriac, peeled

1 carrot, peeled

7 oz (200 g) smoked pancetta
    lardons, fried

3 tablespoons white wine vinegar

2 egg yolks

1 tablespoon plain yogurt

2 bunches of tarragon, chopped

Salt and freshly ground black pepper

Place the pork ribs into a large, deep pan and cover with the water. Add the bay leaves and bring to a boil, then cover and simmer for 1 hour, using a slotted spoon to skim off any foam that forms on the surface as often as you can.

In a food processor, pulse the onions, parsnip, celeriac, and carrot. Add them to the broth and simmer for a further hour.

Remove the ribs from the broth and transfer to a separate dish. When cool enough to handle, remove the meat from the bones and cut into rough chunks. Return the meat to the broth, add the fried pancetta and vinegar, bring back to a boil, and simmer for 5 minutes. Remove from the heat and set aside while you prepare the finishing touches.

Mix the egg yolks with the yogurt and tarragon and season with salt and pepper. Add a few tablespoons of the hot broth to the egg mixture to increase its temperature, then add back to the broth, stirring quickly to avoid the mixture splitting. Serve the broth straight away.

Ciorbă de legume cu gogoşari

Vegetable broth with pickled peppers

Serves 4–6

This light, colorful broth can be made with any combination of vegetables. Don't feel limited by the ingredients list—use anything you have. The peppers pickled in vinegar impart a tangy flavor. You can also use cornichons if they are easier to find.

Heat the oil in a deep pan over medium-high heat. Cook the onion for 8 minutes, or until soft and translucent. Add the carrot and parsnip and continue to cook until the vegetables are golden and starting to caramelize.

Pour the water into the pan and add the celeriac and potatoes. Bring to a simmer and cook for 15 minutes or until the potatoes are just soft. Season lightly with salt and pepper. Add the eggplant, peas, and tomatoes and return to a simmer.

Add the beet, pickled peppers and pickling juice, and chopped herbs. Taste and adjust the seasoning.

For a richer broth, add 2 egg yolks beaten with yogurt (see technique on page 84).

3 tablespoons vegetable oil

1 medium onion, diced

1 carrot, diced

1 parsnip, diced

8½ cups (2 liters) water

¼ large celeriac, diced

2 medium potatoes, sliced

1 eggplant, diced

2 handfuls of fresh peas

1 x 14 oz (400 g) can chopped tomatoes

1 small cooked beet, diced

1 x 12 oz (350 g) jar pickled
    peppers, sliced, plus 3–4
    tablespoons pickling juice

¼ bunch of lovage, chopped

1 bunch of parsley, chopped

1 bunch of dill, chopped

2 egg yolks, beaten with 1 tablespoon
    plain yogurt (optional)

Salt and freshly ground black pepper

CHAPTER FOUR

The main event

Traditional Romanian main courses mostly are stews called *tocană*, *mâncare*, or *ghiveci* and we eat them with pickles, polenta, or dumplings. We also love fruit in savory dishes, whether cooked with meat, stuffed into apples, or as in the famous chicken and quince stew.

Pork and chicken are the traditional meats of choice, but in a country with such a diverse range of resources, it would be impossible not to eat beef, veal, lamb, duck, goose, wild boar, venison, and even bear meat (responsibly hunted). With so many rivers cutting through the landscape, including the mightiest of all—the Danube— fish also plays an important part in our cuisine: usually carp, perch, catfish, shad, pike, salmon, and trout.

The Black Sea is rich in anchovies, which we call *hamsii* and adore fried, as well as mackerel, haddock, sea bream, and some endangered species such as sturgeon and beluga. We used to prepare the caviar at Vâlcov in the Danube Delta, but now the town is part of the Ukraine.

We have a long tradition of eating vegetables and grains. In fact, we eat these more often than meat, be it summer or winter, but especially during Lent. In our Othodox religion, Lent is dotted across the year, including Ash Wednesday, Easter, Advent, important saints' days, and religious ceremonies. We use smoky and tangy flavors to boost these rather austere dishes, making them delicious.

During the hot months of summer the only way to cook is on the grill or in summer kitchens. These look like outdoor sheds with no walls, just a roof, and contain clay ovens and a large homemade grill, where meat, vegetables, and even polenta are cooked over the flames. The kitchen table is moved outside to a shady spot where the food can be enjoyed, under arches of grapevines.

Sarmale

Stuffed cabbage leaves

This is our national dish—sauerkraut cabbage leaves rolled around succulent ground pork, baked in a rich tomato sauce, served with silky polenta, and cooled with a dollop of tangy sour cream.

Sarmale is a celebratory dish and in my family we make it at Christmas and Easter. For enthusiasts, there are seasonal versions using grape, horseradish, linden, or cherry leaves filled with sticky rice and raisins, or even fish baked in huge hollowed-out pumpkins.

The name *Sarmale* comes from the Turkish *sarmak*, meaning roll, and it became part of our culinary repertoire during the hundreds of years spent under the Ottoman empire. Everybody has their own version, passed down by their moms and grandmas, making the recipes very personal.

Makes 30

For the filling:
2 tablespoons vegetable oil
    or sunflower oil
2 onions, diced
2 garlic cloves, sliced
3 tablespoons arborio rice
4 oz (120 g) smoked pancetta,
    finely chopped
12 oz (350 g) ground pork
1 egg, beaten
Salt and freshly ground black pepper

For assembling:
15 whole sauerkraut leaves (see page 186)
¾ cup (7 oz/200 g) shredded
    sauerkraut (store-bought or
    see page 186), drained, plus
    any trimmings from rolling
1 large onion, sliced
1 bunch of thyme, leaves picked
4 bay leaves
6 juniper berries, crushed
2 cups (500 ml) tomato passata or purée
1 cup (250 ml) beef stock

To make the filling, heat the oil in a frying pan over medium heat and soften the onions. Add the garlic, rice, and pancetta, and fry together for 6–7 minutes until the rice is golden, then set aside. In a bowl, mix together the pork and egg then add the onion mixture. Season with salt and pepper and combine well.

To roll the *sarmale*, take one sauerkraut leaf, trim or cut it in half if it's too large, and remove the tough stalk at the end. Take a spoonful of the filling and place it at the edge of the leaf. Roll tightly, tucking in the edges as you go along. Repeat with the remaining leaves.

Preheat the oven to 350°F (180°C). To assemble, line the bottom of a lidded, deep Dutch oven with a layer of shredded sauerkraut, together with half the sliced onion and half the thyme. Cover with a layer of stuffed rolls, tucking the bay leaves in between the rolls. Add a thin layer of shredded sauerkraut, and another layer of rolls. Finish with a layer of shredded sauerkraut and the remaining onion and thyme, then sprinkle over the crushed juniper berries. Pour over the passata and stock.

Cover the pot with aluminum foil and the lid and bake for 1½ hours. Remove the foil and the lid and return to the oven for a further 30 minutes, until the liquid has reduced a little. The *sarmale* will keep in the fridge for 2–3 days, becoming even more delicious by the day. Serve with cooked polenta, sour cream, and slices of hot green chili peppers.

Mici "Littles"

Romanian sour cream meat sausage

These little meaty, garlicky, juicy, melt-in-the-mouth rolls are a Romanian street food staple. So much so, that we even eat them while waiting for the bus to arrive. When the weather turns warm, it's impossible to resist the smoky aromas rising from the *mici* cooked on huge grills set up along the streets. They are usually served on paper plates with a generous dollop of mustard and a slice of crusty white bread to mop up the juices.

Makes 15–20

Ask your butcher to grind the meat together with the fatback for you, so you won't have to grind it separately at home. The fat is key to the juiciness and texture of the *mici*—it can be made with less but the texture will be slightly drier.

Combine all the ingredients except for the oil together in a bowl. Knead by hand to an almost bread-like dough resembling a paste. Refrigerate for at least 1 hour.

Grease a baking sheet or large tray. With wet hands shape about ¼ cup (2 oz/60 g) of the mixture into a chunky little sausage, approximately 4 inches (10 cm) long and 1 inch (2.5 cm) thick. Place onto the prepared tray. Repeat with the remaining mixture then cover and refrigerate for at least 1 hour or, ideally, overnight.

Heat the oil in a large frying pan over medium-high heat and cook the *mici* on all sides, turning them 6 times in total, until browned on the outside and soft and juicy in the middle. Alternatively, cook on a hot grill, brushing with a little oil first. Serve with bread and mustard, if desired.

10½ oz (300 g) ground beef

1 lb 2 oz (500 g) ground pork

7 oz (200 g) pork fatback or lardo, diced and briefly ground in a food processor

3 slices of white bread, soaked in milk

1 garlic bulb, peeled and cloves crushed to a paste

1 teaspoon black pepper

2 teaspoons sweet paprika

1 teaspoon dried thyme

1 teaspoon salt

2 tablespoons sour cream

⅓ cup (80 ml) cold concentrated beef stock made from ½ stock cube dissolved in ⅓ cup (80 ml) hot water

2 tablespoons vegetable oil or sunflower oil, for frying, plus extra for greasing

Musaca de cartofi

Potato moussaka

We took the best parts of both Greek and Turkish moussaka and made our own delicious Romanian version. We use sliced potatoes instead of eggplants, a rich meaty tomato sauce for the filling, and a creamy yogurt and cheese layer on top. My recipe is with ground pork, since my family always preferred it, but some people like to mix pork with beef, or even lamb—especially in the spring, around Easter. Serve it as soon as it's ready, but try it cold the next day, too; it makes for a delicious lunch.

Serves 4

For the filling:

1 tablespoon vegetable oil or sunflower oil

2 onions, finely diced

1 carrot, finely diced

1 lb 2 oz (500 g) ground pork

1 tablespoon sweet paprika

1 x 14 oz (400 g) can chopped tomatoes

1¼ cups (300 ml) tomato passata or purée

Salt and freshly ground black pepper

For the potatoes:

4 medium potatoes

6 cups (1.5 liters) water

For the cheese sauce:

3½ oz (100 g) Cheddar cheese, grated

Generous ½ cup (5 oz/150 g) plain yogurt

2 egg yolks

For assembling:

1 tablespoon (½ oz/15 g) butter

Salt and freshly ground black pepper

To make the filling, heat the oil in a frying pan over medium heat and sauté the onions and carrot for 6–7 minutes. Add the remaining ingredients, season with salt and pepper, and cook for 25 minutes, stirring occasionally, until reduced and thickened.

Meanwhile, peel and slice the potatoes into ⅛ inch- (3 mm-) thick rounds. Bring the water to a boil over high heat and blanch the potatoes for 5 minutes or until just softened. Drain and set aside.

To make the cheese sauce, mix the cheese with the yogurt and egg yolks.

Preheat the oven to 350°F (180°C). Grease a 10 by 7 inch (25 by 18 cm) baking dish with a little of the butter and arrange a layer of potatoes on the base, overlapping the slices slightly. Dot with a little butter and season with salt and pepper, then spread half the filling on top. Arrange another layer of potatoes, dot with butter, and season, then spread the remaining filling on top. Finish with a layer of potatoes and top with the cheese sauce.

Bake for 30–35 minutes and serve with a simple tomato salad.

Mere cu şuncă

Apples stuffed with ham

Stuffed vegetables and fruit are a staple of Romanian cuisine, particularly in Muntenia (or Wallachia) to the south of the Carpathian Mountains. This is a region of soft hills, vast plains, and large fruit orchards, and most of our apples come from this part of the country. I couldn't have chosen a more enticing dish for you— both easy to make and spectacular to put on the table.

Serves 4

8 firm apples
7 oz (200 g) ham, finely diced
1 medium red onion, finely diced
1½ oz/40 g Romanian telemea cheese
    or feta, grated, plus extra to serve
¼ cup (1½ oz/40 g) breadcrumbs
2 tablespoons (1 oz/30 g) butter
Scant 1 cup (200 ml) cider
½ bunch of rosemary
Salt and freshly ground black pepper

Preheat the oven to 400°F (200°C). To prepare the apples cut a "lid" from the top of each apple, about one-third down the fruit. Carefully core the apples and scoop out some of the flesh, leaving the bottom and the walls intact. Finely dice the scooped-out apple flesh, combine with the ham, onion, and cheese, and season with salt and pepper. Fill each apple with the mixture, then top with the breadcrumbs and a pat of butter. Replace the apple lids.

Place the apples into a shallow baking pan or round baking dish. Pour the cider into the pan, add the rosemary, and bake for 30 minutes.

Serve alongside braised cabbage or as an appetizer with a sprinkling of extra cheese.

Tocană de fasole cu ciolan afumat

Smoked ham hock and lima bean casserole

Ask any Romanian about their favorite food and they will most likely mention this casserole. It is a very satisfying dish, the ham hock being a wonderful piece of meat to slow cook, and the herby lima beans perfect for carrying the smoky flavors. The aromas that come from the oven while this is cooking are enough to whet your appetite and make you dream of traveling through Romania, exploring all of its culinary riches. Enjoy this dish with family and friends for an utterly rewarding dinner.

Preheat the oven to 350°F (180°C). Soak the ham hock in cold water for 15 minutes, then drain and pat dry with a dish towel. Heat 1 tablespoon of the oil in a large Dutch oven over medium heat and brown the ham hock on all sides. Remove from the pot and set aside.

Add the remaining oil, onion, and garlic to the Dutch oven and cook for 6–7 minutes. Pour over the ale and a scant ½ cup (100 ml) of water then return the ham hock to the pot.

Wrap the Dutch oven in aluminum foil and cover with the lid, ensuring no steam can escape. Place in the oven and cook for 2 hours.

Carefully remove the foil and add the tomatoes, lima beans, and thyme, and season with pepper, and salt, if using. Return to the oven, uncovered, for a further 20 minutes.

Serve hot in a large dish in the center of the table, with beet salad and pickles.

Serves 4

2–2¼ lb (900 g–1 kg) smoked ham hock
2 tablespoons vegetable oil
    or sunflower oil
1 onion, roughly chopped
4 garlic cloves, roughly chopped
1 x 12 oz (330 ml) bottle dark ale
1 x 14 oz (400 g) can chopped tomatoes
2 x 14 oz (400 g) cans lima beans
2 teaspoons dried thyme
Freshly ground black pepper
Salt (optional)

Ostropel de Oltenia

Chicken in garlic tomato sauce with polenta dumplings

Serves 4

For the chicken:

2 tablespoons vegetable oil
    or sunflower oil
8 chicken thighs
3 cups (750 ml) tomato passata or purée
Scant 1 cup (200 ml) chicken stock
5–6 garlic cloves, crushed

For the dumplings:

2 cups (500 ml) chicken stock
1¼ cups (5 oz/150 g) self-rising flour
Scant ½ cup (2 oz/60 g) coarse polenta
2 tablespoons olive oil
3½ tablespoons water
2 eggs, beaten
Salt

To serve:

2 garlic cloves, finely sliced
¼ bunch of parsley, chopped

This is a dish with soul and temperament. It takes me on a journey back to the land of my grandfather, Gheorghe, and great-grandfather, Haralambie. They were from Oltenia to the south of the Carpathian mountains, an area known worldwide for its traditional hand-woven rugs and tapestries. In Romania, Oltenians are known (and often teased) for their short tempers and passionate nature, and this dish is a bit like them—quick and fiery.

To cook the chicken, heat the oil in a deep frying pan over high heat and brown the chicken thighs for a few minutes on each side. Pour in the passata and stock, add the crushed garlic, and simmer for 40 minutes or until the chicken is cooked through.

Meanwhile, make the dumplings—ideally they will be ready at the same time as the chicken. Pour the stock into a large pan over medium heat. Combine the remaining ingredients, along with a pinch of salt, until the mixture is thick enough to just drop off the spoon. Use a tablespoon to drop the dumpling mixture into the hot stock. Leave to cook for 8 minutes. Once cooked, they will be soft on the outside and firm on the inside. Remove the dumplings from the stock and set aside until the chicken is cooked.

Add the dumplings to the frying pan with the chicken, evenly coating them with the sauce, and cook for a further 2–3 minutes. Serve immediately, sprinkled with the garlic and parsley.

Muşchiuleţ Sibian

Stuffed Sibiu pork tenderloin with pickled mushrooms

Sibiu is a stunning city in Transylvania, the largest and wealthiest of all fortified towns built by the Saxons between the twelfth and fifteenth centuries. Strolling down its narrow alleys, it feels like a fairytale town with its colorful houses and imposing buildings. In southern Transylvania, we have a network of more than 250 Saxon villages and towns forming an incredible heritage that is worth preserving and exploring.

This dish is my own personal madeleine, taking me back to special occasion family dinners in the elegant restaurants of Sibiu. I find it wonderful served for a Sunday dinner with a side of tangy pickled mushrooms.

To butterfly the pork tenderloin, place the pork on a chopping board. Holding a knife perpendicular to the board, slice the tenderloin in half lengthwise, making sure that you don't cut all the way through to the other side. Open it like a book, cover with plastic wrap, and pound it with a rolling pin or meat hammer.

Remove the plastic wrap, season the pork with salt and pepper, and cover with the sliced cheese, then with the ham. Roll tightly, then tie with string at the ends, in the middle, and across the length.

Heat the oil and butter in a large frying pan, preferably with a lid, over medium heat and carefully brown the tenderloin evenly on all sides for 7–8 minutes. Add the wine and put the lid on or cover with foil. Turn the heat down to low and cook for a further 30 minutes. Set the pan aside to allow the meat to rest while you make the pickled mushrooms.

To make the pickled mushrooms, heat the oil in a separate pan over medium heat and cook the onion and mushrooms until soft and slightly caramelized and any liquid has reduced. Combine the vinegar with the remaining ingredients, season with salt and pepper, and pour over the mushrooms. Toss everything together and cook for a further 2–3 minutes.

Remove the string from the tenderloin and slice into thick slices. Transfer to a serving dish, spoon over some of the juice from the pan, and serve with the pickled mushrooms and chopped parsley on the side.

Serves 4

For the pork tenderloin:
1 pork tenderloin, around 1 lb 2 oz (500 g)
6 slices Gouda cheese or
    Romanian cascaval
4–6 slices good-quality ham
2 tablespoons vegetable oil
    or sunflower oil
4 tablespoons (2 oz/60 g) butter
½ cup (120 ml) white wine
Salt and freshly ground black pepper

For the pickled mushrooms:
3 tablespoons vegetable oil
    or sunflower oil
1 onion, finely sliced
9 oz (250 g) white button
    mushrooms, sliced
¼ cup (60 ml) white wine vinegar
½ teaspoon mustard
Pinch of ground nutmeg
½ bunch of parsley, finely chopped,
    plus extra to serve
Salt and freshly ground black pepper

Pârjoale

Breaded meatballs

Makes about 12

For the meatballs:

1 lb 2 oz (500 g) ground pork

2 onions, finely diced

4 garlic cloves, crushed to a paste

1 slice of white bread, soaked
    in milk and squeezed

1 egg, beaten

2 teaspoons black pepper

2 teaspoons salt

2 bunches of dill, finely chopped

For frying:

1¼ cup (5 oz/150 g) all-purpose flour

Vegetable oil or sunflower oil

These meatballs have a truly evocative name in Romanian—
a pârjoli means to burn quickly and to the ground, which is
pretty much the way you need to fry them in the pan. Okay,
maybe don't burn them, but aim for a dark, extra-crisp exterior.
Serve them with mashed potatoes and pickles in the winter, or
with garden peas in the summer.

To make the meatballs, combine all of the ingredients and mix well
to an almost paste-like consistency. Refrigerate for 1 hour. With wet
hands, take ¼ cup (2 oz/60 g) of the mixture and shape into balls,
flattening each slightly into an oval shape.

Place the flour in a shallow dish. Pat each meatball with a little
flour on all sides, pressing lightly. Cover the bottom of a large frying
pan with a thin layer of oil. Try to snuggle all of the meatballs into
the pan in one go. Fry on medium heat for 10–15 minutes, turning
frequently, until extra crispy.

Pastramă de oaie cu mujdei

Pastrami-style roasted leg of lamb served with farmhouse
potatoes and garlic vinaigrette.

Is this a mistake? Surely pastrami is made of beef and definitely not
roasted. Rumor has it that it was a Romanian-Jew who took the
original lamb *pastramă* recipe to New York, where he offered the
recipe to one of the Jewish shops in return for a favor. They took it,
adapted it, and made it famous. In Romania, we still use the original
recipe, salting and curing the meat first, then slicing it in long strips
and cooking on a grill. We serve it with extra garlic sauce and a side
dish of crushed potatoes. My recipe below is inspired by the flavors
of this traditional dish, without having to wait for weeks to eat it.

To make the spice rub, crush the garlic in a pestle and mortar, or
pulse in a food processor. Add all of the remaining ingredients, except
for the oil, and grind together. Pour in the oil and grind to a paste.
Rub the paste into the lamb leg, gently and patiently, then cover and
refrigerate overnight.

The following day, preheat the oven to 350°F (180°C). Pierce the
lamb all over with a knife and push the halved garlic cloves into the
holes. Place in a roasting pan, pour over the stock and wine, and add
the rosemary. Cover with aluminum foil and roast for 1½ hours, then
remove the foil and roast for a further 15 minutes or until there is a
dark crust enveloping the lamb (it will be well-done, closer in taste to
the traditional *pastramă*).

To make the potatoes, put them in a large pan and cover with
water. Bring to a boil and cook until tender but not soft. Drain and set
aside. When the lamb is almost ready, heat the oil in a frying pan over
medium heat, add the pancetta and onion, and fry for 10 minutes.
Add the potatoes and toss, slightly crushing them in the process using
a fork.

Place the leg of lamb on the table as the centerpiece and serve
with the potatoes and a drizzle of garlic vinaigrette.

Serves 6

3 lb 8 oz (1.6 kg) leg of lamb, bone-in

For the spice rub:

6 garlic cloves, peeled

4 teaspoons dried thyme or winter savory

4 teaspoons smoked paprika

2 teaspoons dried coriander

2 teaspoons juniper berries, crushed

1 tablespoon ground black pepper

2 teaspoons salt

2 teaspoons dark brown sugar

¼ cup (60 ml) olive oil or rapeseed oil

For roasting:

4 garlic cloves, peeled and halved

1 cup (250 ml) lamb stock

1½ cups (350 ml) red wine

1 bunch of rosemary

For the potatoes:

7 oz (200 g) new potatoes,
  halved or quartered

1 tablespoon vegetable, sunflower,
  or rapeseed oil

3½ oz (100 g) smoked pancetta, sliced

1 onion, sliced

Garlic vinaigrette (see page 209), to serve

Pilaf cu pui și ciuperci

Oven-baked pearl barley pilaf with chicken and mushrooms

Serves 4

3 tablespoons vegetable oil
   or sunflower oil
3 lb 5 oz (1.5 kg) whole chicken, cut into
   pieces (breast, thighs, drumsticks,
   back, neck), bone-in and skin-on
2 onions, chopped
1½ cups (10½ oz/300 g) pearl
   barley (ideally whole-grain)
¼ celeriac, diced
2–3 celery stalks, diced
1 carrot, diced
1 red pepper, diced
1 x 14 oz (400 g) can chopped tomatoes
7 oz (200 g) white button
   mushrooms, quartered
2½ cups (600 ml) chicken stock
2 tablespoons (1 oz/30 g) butter,
   roughly chopped
Salt and freshly ground black pepper
1 bunch of parsley, roughly
   chopped, to serve

This dish is unfussy to cook and a joy eat, with a gentle buttery texture and comforting aromas. I find it a lot of fun to use a whole chicken cut into different pieces, so you never know what you will get, it's like a chicken-roulette. You need to be generous with the salt; it will make the flavors stand out. In some parts of the country it's called Serbian pilaf, probably because of the added sweet pepper since Serbia is well known for the quality of its vegetables.

Preheat the oven to 325°F (160°C). Heat the oil in a large deep Dutch oven, preferably with a lid, over medium heat and brown the chicken pieces on all sides. Remove the chicken and transfer to a plate.

Add the onions to the pot and cook for 10 minutes, then add the pearl barley and stir to coat the grains with the oil, cooking for a few more minutes. Add the diced vegetables, along with the tomatoes, mushrooms, and stock, season with salt and pepper, and gently stir combine. Return the chicken to the pot, then cover with aluminum foil, and place the lid on top.

Place in the oven and cook for 40 minutes, then carefully remove the lid and foil and cook for a further 10 minutes. Remove from the oven and dot with the butter.

Sprinkle with parsley and serve hot, accompanied with tomato slices or lettuce.

Gutui cu carne

Pan-fried chicken with caramelized quince

This dish originates from the Banat region in the south-west of Romania. It has an incredibly diverse history, from Avar tribes, to Turks and Austrians, and even Swabians. One style in particular stands out: meat dishes with fruits, often made with a light caramelized sauce that brings out their delicate perfume.

Heat the butter in a deep frying pan over medium heat and fry the quince for 2 minutes on each side. Add the rum and cook for a further 3–4 minutes, then transfer to a plate.

Heat the oil in the same pan. Coat the chicken legs in the flour, then brown in the oil for 10 minutes, turning frequently. Set aside.

In a clean pan, heat the sugar on medium heat until it melts and begins to change color. Carefully add the water while stirring continuously, then return the chicken legs to the pan. Cover and cook for 15–20 minutes over medium heat, or until the chicken is cooked through, adding a little more water if the sauce reduces too quickly. Add the quince, rosemary, and salt to the pan and cook for a further 5 minutes.

Remove from the heat and serve. If you are new to this style of dish, first try it by removing the chicken and quince from the sauce—both will have a light, shiny coating of sauce. When you realize that you like it, you can add some more...or all of it.

Serves 2

4 tablespoons (2 oz/60 g) butter
3 quinces, peeled and sliced into
    ¾ inch (2 cm) wedges
2 tablespoons rum
1 tablespoon vegetable oil or sunflower oil
2 chicken legs
Generous ¾ cup (3½ oz/100 g)
    all-purpose flour
2 tablespoons sugar
Scant ½ cup (100 ml) water
½ bunch of rosemary
1 teaspoon salt

Drob de Paște

Lamb terrine

Serves 12

For the crêpes:

Generous 1½ cups
(7 oz/200 g) all-
purpose flour

2 eggs

2½ cups (600 ml)
whole milk

1 teaspoon salt

Vegetable oil or sunflower
oil, for frying

Butter, for crêpes

For the terrine:

2 tablespoons vegetable
oil or sunflower oil

9 oz (250 g) lamb or
chicken livers

1 tablespoon white
wine vinegar

¼ cup (2 oz/60 g) yogurt

5 oz (150 g) diced lamb

1 lb 5 oz (600 g) good-
quality ground lamb

4 bunches of scallions,
green tops only, sliced

4–5 garlic cloves,
finely chopped

5 eggs

2 bunches of fresh parsley,
finely chopped

1 bunch of fresh dill,
finely chopped

Salt and freshly ground
black pepper

For assembling:

3 eggs, soft-boiled
and peeled

Melted butter, for
greasing and crêpes

This is our hero dish at Easter, the only time when Romanians eat lamb. Easter is the most important celebration in our Orthodox calendar, and a time when we return home to the heart of our families. At midnight on the eve of Easter we gather at church to cheer the resurrection of Christ. *Cristos a înviat*—"Christ is risen" says the priest. *Adevart a înviat*—"Indeed he is risen"—we all reply in one unanimous voice growing tall towards the sky. We light candles for one another, turning the streets into a sea of flickering holy lights. It's a powerful and emotional spectacle, but by now we are all thinking of food, so we go back home, exchange dyed boiled eggs, and eat *drob*.

The traditional recipe is exclusively made with offal, and the outside casing is a beautiful lamb lace fat, which unfortunately is hard to find in stores. I chose to make my version with ground and diced lamb and liver for binding everything together. The casing is made of crêpes, but you can also use pastry dough.

Begin the preparations 1 day in advance, so the terrine can rest in the fridge overnight.

To make the crêpes, combine the flour, eggs, milk, and salt in a bowl and refrigerate for 1 hour. Heat a tablespoon of oil in a large frying pan. Add enough batter to thinly and evenly coat the base of the pan, tilting the pan to move the mixture around. Leave to cook for about 30 seconds until golden underneath, then ease a spatula under the crêpe to lift and flip it over. Add a pat of butter each time you flip. Cook for a further 30 seconds, then transfer to a plate to cool. Repeat with the remaining batter.

To make the terrine, heat 1 tablespoon of the oil in a frying pan and heat to its smoking point. Add the livers and fry for 2 minutes on each side. Add the vinegar and toss for 1 minute. Set aside to cool, then blend with the yogurt in a food processor.

Try to remove as much of the white sinew from the diced lamb as you can (I sometimes dice it again if the butcher preferred chunkier pieces). In the same pan, heat the remaining oil and add the diced and ground lamb. Cook on medium-high heat for around 15 minutes or until the juices reduce. Set aside to cool, then combine with the liver mixture in a large bowl. Add the remaining ingredients, season with salt and pepper, and stir to combine. The mixture should look homogeneous—if it doesn't, add more yogurt or another egg and stir again.

Preheat the oven to 350°F (180°C). Grease a 12 by 3½ inch (30 by 9 cm) terrine dish with a little butter. Arrange the crêpes to cover the base and sides of the pan, allowing them to hang over the edges. It doesn't have to be very precise, just make sure every bit of the dish is covered. Press half of the lamb mixture into the terrine dish. Add the whole soft-boiled eggs in a row, then add the remaining lamb mixture, pressing gently so as not to burst the eggs but firmly enough to get rid of any air bubbles.

Cover the terrine with the over-hanging crêpes, so that they meet in the middle. Brush with the melted butter. Bake for 40 minutes then refrigerate overnight. Serve the terrine as a cold starter, one thick slice per person, with lettuce and mustard.

Momițe

Polenta-coated sweetbreads

Coating the sweetbreads creates a contrast between the crisp exterior and the rich, creamy interior. They are fragile to handle, so don't worry if they fall apart. You will find them served as delicacies in any traditional restaurant in Romania, alongside dishes of liver, brain, bone marrow, and ox tongue, all prepared with exquisite mastery. They have a European familiarity, being considered the finest food in many restaurants from Stockholm to Lyon, Budapest to Bucharest.

Prepare a bowl of cold water. Rinse the sweetbreads under cold running water and place in a pan over medium heat. Add the water and vinegar and simmer for up to 10 minutes or until relatively firm to the touch. Immediately transfer the sweetbreads to the bowl of water and carefully remove the thin layers of skin and any sinew.

Place the egg and polenta into separate shallow dishes. Dip the sweetbreads first into the egg and then into the polenta.

Melt the butter in a shallow pan over low heat and add the oil. Gently slide the sweetbreads into the pan and cook for 3–4 minutes on each side, or until the outside has turned golden brown. Remove with a slotted spoon and drain on paper towels.

Spoon over a little garlic vinaigrette and serve with garden peas, if desired.

Serves 4

10½ oz (300 g) lamb sweetbreads
1¼ cups (300 ml) water
1 tablespoon apple cider vinegar
1 egg, beaten
½ cup (2½ oz/75 g) coarse polenta
2 tablespoons (1 oz/30 g) butter
1 tablespoon vegetable oil or sunflower oil
Garlic vinaigrette (see page 209), to serve

Rață pe varză

Duck legs with baked sauerkraut

The beauty of this dish is that it is impossible to overcook. If you like duck but are afraid to cook with it, then fear no more, this recipe is for you. The oven will do all the work, while your job will be to set up the dining ambience, open the wine, light the candles, and put the music on. I like to serve duck with tangy sauerkraut because it cuts through the delicious duck fat without the need for any acidic fruit sauces.

Serves 4

2 tablespoons vegetable oil
    or sunflower oil
4 duck legs
½ bunch of thyme
1 onion, finely sliced
2½ cups (1 lb 5 oz/600 g) shredded
    sauerkraut (store-bought or
    see page 186), drained
¼ cup (2 oz/60 g) tomato paste
Scant 1 cup (200 ml) chicken stock
Salt and freshly ground black pepper
Green chili peppers, sliced
    (optional), to serve

Preheat the oven to 350°F (180°C). Massage 1 tablespoon of the oil into the duck legs, then sprinkle with salt and pepper. Arrange the thyme in a roasting pan in a single layer, then place the duck legs on top and roast for 1¼ hours.

Meanwhile, heat the remaining oil in a frying pan over low heat and gently cook the onion for 5 minutes. Add the sauerkraut, tomato paste, and stock, stir to combine, and cook for a further 10 minutes.

Carefully remove the pan from the oven. Remove the duck legs, spoon out half of the fat, then add the sauerkraut mixture to the pan. Place the legs on top, then return to the oven for a further 15 minutes or until the cabbage has caramelized on top.

Serve sprinkled with green chili peppers, if desired.

Limbă cu măsline

Poached ox tongue with olive salsa

This dish benefits from a long and slow simmer, which brings
out the richness of the flavors and smoothness of the texture.
It is a phenomenal sight, reminding us that once committed to
eating meat, we should waste nothing. It wouldn't be sustainable
otherwise to either farmer or buyer. I was brought up to appreciate
offal, and this poached ox tongue was a regular dish in our family.
I dared to modernize it and turned the traditional stew into a cold
lunch, served with an olive salsa. Sorry mom!

Warm some water in a kettle or on the stove. Put the ox tongue,
onion, bay leaves, and juniper berries into a deep pan over low heat
and cover with the hot water. Cover and simmer for 2 hours.

Meanwhile, make the salsa. With the exception of the olives, mix
all the ingredients together and pulse briefly in a food processor until
roughly chopped. Transfer to a bowl and add the olives.

After 2 hours, turn off the heat and leave the ox tongue to cool in
the water before transferring to a chopping board. To peel the tongue,
make an incision at its base and push your finger under this outer
layer all the way up to the tip. It should come off fairly easily, but if
not, you can use a knife to help.

Cut the tongue into thin slices and serve with the salsa as an
appetizer, or add steamed potatoes for a good lunch. The next day,
you can use it as a sandwich filling as you would with corned beef.

Serves 8–10

1 ox tongue

1 onion, peeled but left whole

3 bay leaves

4–5 juniper berries, lightly crushed

For the olive salsa:

2 garlic cloves

4–5 slices of sun-dried tomatoes

¼ bunch of parsley

3 tablespoons small capers

¼ cup (60 ml) olive oil or rapeseed oil

1 tablespoon apple cider
    vinegar or lemon juice

½ cup (3½ oz/100 g) mixed olives,
    pitted and quartered

Rasol de vacă

Osso buco with vegetables, dill oil, and horseradish sauce

Serves 4

2 tablespoons vegetable oil
    or sunflower oil

1 onion, diced

1 celery stick, sliced

6 cups (1.5 liters) water

2 lb 4 oz (1 kg) veal shanks

3 bay leaves

6–7 juniper berries, lightly crushed

2–3 medium carrots, peeled and
    quartered lengthwise, or 2 bunches
    of baby rainbow carrots

9 oz (250 g) green beans,
    trimmed and halved

For the dill oil:
½ bunch of dill
¼ cup (60 ml) rapeseed oil
Zest of 1 lemon

For the horseradish sauce:
¼ horseradish root, grated
2 tablespoons plain yogurt
2 garlic cloves, crushed
Salt and freshly ground black pepper

This *rasol* is an extremely satisfying dish without relying on rich sauces to fill you up. Everything comes together at the same time in a knock-out dish that is homey and flavorful. It comes with a choice of a refreshing dill oil, which I love for its light bitter undertones, or with a classic peppery horseradish sauce. Personally, I'm quite greedy and I like to use a little bit of both.

Heat the oil in a deep pan large enough to hold the meat. Add the onion and celery and cook over medium heat for 8–10 minutes. Add the water and bring to a boil, then put the veal into the pan with the bay leaves and juniper berries. Bring everything to a boil, then turn the heat to low, cover the pan, and simmer for 1½ hours.

Meanwhile, make the dill oil: put all of the ingredients into a food processor, pulse a few times, and reserve in a small dish.

For the horseradish sauce: pulse all the ingredients together in a food processor and season to taste with salt and pepper.

After 1½ hours, add the carrots and green beans to the pan and cook for 10–12 minutes or until the vegetables are just softened but retaining their crunch. Remove everything from the pan with a slotted spoon and transfer to a serving platter. Drizzle over the dill oil and dot with the horseradish sauce.

Saramură de pește

Romanian mackerel bouillabaisse

This is my image of a summer vacation in the Danube Delta: the water, sun, and a grill. The magnificent Danube river unites with the Black Sea in the wildest and second largest delta in Europe. Vacationing here also means a full commitment to eating fish, since everything is made with it: fish dumplings, fish balls, *borș*, fish stuffed peppers or cabbage leaves, fish *rasol*, or steak. This *saramură* would normally be made with carp belly, perch, catfish, or pike—all amazing freshwater fish common in our rivers—but since I moved abroad I've been using fresh mackerel. It is perfect for grilling and for carrying through the flavor of the sea.

Bring 1 cup (250 ml) water to a boil in a large pan over low heat and heat a griddle pan over high heat. Add the vinegar, salt, bay leaves, garlic, and chili to the pan with the water and keep hot. Pat the mackerel dry using a dish towel and sprinkle with salt on both sides. When the griddle pan is smoking-hot, add the fish (no need for oil) and cook for 2–3 minutes on each side until the skin is almost charred, which will add a little smokiness to the overall flavor.

Transfer the fish to a deep baking pan and pour over the hot brined water. Leave to infuse for 5 minutes.

To serve, place each fish onto a serving plate, sprinkle over the scallions, then spoon over a little of the brine along with some of the chilies and garlic. (The brine is there mainly for seasoning purposes.) You don't have to eat the skin if you don't like the idea, but I love the light bitterness of it, and it melts in the mouth.

Traditionally, this dish is served with Creamy Polenta (see page 209). I suggest making the polenta first and keeping it warm in the pan, while you prepare the brine and grill the fish. The whole process is done in less than 10 minutes.

Serves 2

3 tablespoons apple cider vinegar

2 teaspoons salt, plus extra for sprinkling

3 bay leaves

2 garlic cloves, finely sliced

2 green chili peppers, sliced into rounds

2 whole mackerel (about 12 oz/350 g), with or without the heads

3 scallions, green tops only, sliced

Hamsii pané cu mujdei

Polenta-coated anchovies with Romanian garlic sauce

For me, there is nothing quite like a plateful of crispy, zingy, golden fried fish, set in the middle of the table for a quick snack. In our kitchen, there was always a jar of *mujdei* next to the plate for drizzling on the fish. It's not going to be a formal dinner, since the anchovies are best eaten using your fingers, but it happily brings friends together for a chat and a beer.

At home we fry the anchovies whole, but you can ask your fishmonger to clean, gut, and prepare them for you. Once prepared, sprinkle a little salt on each side and set aside for 10–15 minutes. Mix the flour and polenta together in a shallow dish. Heat the oil in a frying pan over high heat, then turn the temperature down to medium. Roll each fish in the flour mixture and fry for 2–3 minutes on each side. Serve, drizzled with the garlic sauce, as a snack or appetizer.

Serves 4

15 anchovies
¾ cup (3½ oz/100 g) polenta
½ cup (2 oz/60 g) all-purpose flour
⅓ cup (80 ml) vegetable oil or sunflower oil
1 quantity garlic sauce (see page 209)
Salt

Plachie de păstrăv

Baked trout with onions and peppers

We are very fond of trout and this beautiful fish can be found in the quick flowing, shallow mountain rivers of the Carpathian mountains. Some like to cure the fish, wrap it in pine branches, and cold-smoke it—we call that a "trout lute," because of the shape of the wrapped fish. My *plachie* uses fresh trout, surrounded by sweet and tangy tomatoes and onions, which reduce in the oven to a flavorful sauce. It's quite a spectacular dish to put on the table.

Preheat the oven to 400°F (200°C). Put the oil, onions, peppers, garlic, and bay leaves in a deep ceramic baking dish and combine well. Bake for 40 minutes, stirring once. Carefully remove the dish from the oven, pour in the wine and vinegar, add the salt, and combine well. Place the trout in the center of the dish, tucking it in among the onions and peppers. Turn the oven down to 350°F (180°C) and bake for a further 30 minutes. Serve with a generous sprinkling of parsley, alongside steamed potatoes or a good dollop of cooked polenta, if desired.

Serves 4

⅓ cup (80 ml) vegetable oil or sunflower oil
4 large onions, finely sliced
3 red peppers, finely sliced
3 garlic cloves, crushed
2 bay leaves
Scant ½ cup (100 ml) white wine
1 tablespoon apple cider vinegar
1 teaspoon salt
1 whole trout (around 14 oz/400 g), head on, gutted and cleaned
½ bunch of parsley, chopped

Pilaf cu prune afumate

Pilaf with smoked prunes and caramelized leeks

This is a testimony to the Persian and Turkish influence in Romanian cooking, where fruit is used in savory dishes. A pilaf is the only traditional way we eat rice, and I love mine with caramelized onions or leeks on top.

After the hot Romanian summer we preserve the surplus of fruit not only by making jams and compotes, but also by sun-drying and cold-smoking. They are more versatile this way, and this pilaf is a joy of textures and flavors. The natural sweetness and smokiness of the prunes, the reassuring presence of the buttery rice, and the crispiness of the leeks come together in a comforting dish that will banish your hunger without the need for meat.

To make the pilaf, heat the oil in a pan over medium heat and sauté the onion. Add the rice and cook for 2–3 minutes, stirring to coat with the oil. Add the wine and cook for a further 3 minutes, then add the stock, cover, and cook for a further 10–15 minutes until the rice is just beginning to soften.

Meanwhile, make the caramelized leeks. Heat the oil in a frying pan over medium-high heat and add the leeks and sugar. Cook until the leeks are dark-golden in color, stirring every minute or so.

When the rice is softened, add the prunes and cook for a further 15 minutes. Season with salt and pepper, remove from the heat, and set aside for 2 minutes, then add the butter and stir well to combine. Serve immediately with the caramelized leeks on top.

Serves 2 generously

For the pilaf:

1 tablespoon vegetable oil or sunflower oil

1 onion, sliced

¾ cup (5 oz/150 g) basmati rice

Scant ½ cup (100 ml) white wine

1¼ cups (300 ml) vegetable stock

½ cup (3½ oz/100 g) hot smoked prunes (see page 208)

2 tablespoons (1 oz/30 g) butter

Salt and freshly ground black pepper

For the caramelized leeks:

2 tablespoons vegetable oil or sunflower oil

1 leek, sliced

1 teaspoon sugar

Sărmăluțe în foi de viță

Grape leaves stuffed with sticky rice and raisins

This is a lighter, summery take on our celebratory stuffed cabbage dish (see page 88). Even without meat this is still a gratifying dish, and its sweet-and-sour double act will almost certainly make you fall in love with it. We cook this in large pots, and eat it family style from the center of the table, sparking debates about tips and ideas on how to cook it best. My aunt Mariana makes the best *sărmăluțe* in our family—she has that magic touch we all try to replicate.

Makes 25–30

25–30 grape leaves, rinsed

For the rice:
1 tablespoon vegetable oil or sunflower oil
1 onion, finely diced
¾ cup (5 oz/150 g) arborio rice
½ cup (120 ml) white wine
1 cup (250 ml) vegetable stock
1 teaspoon salt
½ cup (3½ oz/100 g) raisins
Zest and juice of 1 lemon
1 teaspoon ground fennel

For the sauce:
⅔ cup (150 ml) water
3 cups (750 ml) tomato passata or purée
2 tablespoons apple cider vinegar
1 teaspoon salt
2 medium tomatoes, chopped

To prepare the rice, heat the oil in a large frying pan over medium heat and cook the onion for 8–10 minutes. Add the rice, coating it with the oil, and cook for a further 3 minutes. Pour over the wine and stock, add the salt, and reduce the heat to low. Cover and simmer for 30 minutes, stirring occasionally. The rice filling needs to be sticky but not watery. Add the raisins, lemon zest and juice, and ground fennel and combine well. Set aside to cool.

To make the sauce, combine all the ingredients, except the chopped tomatoes, in a bowl. Spread the chopped tomatoes and 1 tablespoon of the sauce onto the bottom of a deep ovenproof ceramic dish.

Preheat the oven to 325°F (160°C). Spoon around 2 tablespoons (1 oz/30 g) of the rice filling (the quantity will depend on the size of the leaf) into the center of one of the grape leaves. Roll the leaf gently, tucking in the sides as you go. Place into the ceramic dish and repeat with the remaining leaves. Pour the remaining sauce over the leaves, cover with aluminum foil, and bake for 25 minutes.

Serve immediately, or refrigerate overnight and reheat in batches.

Piperchi

Peppers—fricassée style

This dish is specific to Dobrogea in the south-east of Romania, where there are still a few clusters of Macedo-Romanian communities who live by their traditions. They are famous for their hospitality and their food, feeding you a multitude of dishes that will burst your belt while they sing songs and play music between courses. The parties are epic! A breakfast can easily turn into lunch, and carry on into dinner.

Heat the oil in a large frying pan over medium heat and fry the peppers for 5 minutes. Add the passata and tomato paste and simmer for 20 minutes, or until the peppers are just soft. Stir in the cheese, cherry tomatoes, all of the herbs, and season with salt and pepper. If you are using the eggs, stir them in now. Cook for a further minute. Remove from the heat, and serve sprinkled with black pepper and a little more cheese.

Serves 4

2 tablespoons vegetable oil
    or sunflower oil
4 large peppers of different
    colors, thinly sliced
2 cups (500 ml) tomato passata or purée
Scant ½ cup (3½ oz/100 g) tomato paste
4 oz (120 g) Cheddar cheese,
    grated, plus extra to serve
3–4 cherry tomatoes, halved
¼ bunch of thyme, leaves picked
¼ bunch of sage, roughly chopped
¼ bunch of dill, roughly chopped
2 eggs, beaten (optional)
Salt and freshly ground black pepper

Brașovence

Breaded crêpes with mushroom filling

If you are lucky enough to visit Romania, I urge you to go to Brașov and indulge in these breaded crêpes filled with mushrooms. Then go to the Black Church—not to confess how many crêpes you've eaten, but to see its outstanding collection of Anatolian carpets. Invasions from Tatars and Turks and a fire in the 17th century almost destroyed the church and its nickname comes from the blackened, fire-damaged walls. Its imposing Gothic style was meant to impress people and convert them to Catholicism, but the Reformation of the Saxon communities in Transylvania turned it Into a Lutheran church. In my opinion, both the church and the crêpes deserve a thorough study.

Serves 4–6

For the crêpes:
Generous 1½ cups (7 oz/200 g)
    all-purpose flour
2 eggs
2¼ cups (550 ml) whole milk
1 teaspoon salt
Vegetable oil or sunflower oil, for frying

For the filling:
2 tablespoons vegetable oil
    or sunflower oil
2 onions, finely chopped
9 oz (250 g) mushrooms, finely chopped
Salt and freshly ground black pepper

For the coating:
2 eggs, beaten
Generous ¾ cups (3½ oz/100 g)
    all-purpose flour
¾ cup (3½ oz/100 g) breadcrumbs

To serve:
Sour cream or plain yogurt (optional)

To make the crêpes, combine the flour, eggs, milk, and salt in a bowl and refrigerate for 1 hour. Heat a tablespoon of oil in a large frying pan. Add enough batter to thinly and evenly coat the base of the pan, tilting the pan to move the mixture around. Leave to cook for about 30 seconds until golden underneath, then ease a spatula under the crêpe to lift and flip it over. Cook for a further 30 seconds, then transfer to a plate to cool. Repeat with the remaining batter.

To make the filling, heat the oil in large frying pan over medium heat and soften the onions. Add the mushrooms, season with salt and pepper, and cook for 30 minutes until the mixture resembles a rough paste. Set aside in a bowl to cool, then briefly pulse in a food processor to a coarse paste.

Spread 2 teaspoons of the mushroom filling onto one crêpe, then bring the sides to almost meet in the middle. Roll the crêpe and place seam-side down onto a tray. Repeat with the remaining crêpes and filling.

To make the coating, place the eggs, flour, and breadcrumbs into separate shallow dishes. Cover the base of a large frying pan with a thin layer of oil and place over medium heat. Holding the crêpes by both ends, quickly dip them into the egg, then the flour, and then the breadcrumbs and place seam-side down into the frying pan. Cook until the outsides are golden brown, turning a few times to brown evenly. Drain the crêpes of any excess oil on paper towels.

Serve warm on their own or with spoonfuls of sour cream or yogurt.

Mâncare de castraveți acri

Pickled cucumber ragout

Pickles and fermented vegetables add a lot of character to main dishes. My family has a particular fondness for this pickled-cucumber ragout, especially during the numerous Lent days dotted around the year. It is quick to make, satisfying, and goes well with a slice of thick bread or a little polenta on the side to soak up the sauce. No matter how you choose to eat it, it brings joy to days that may look rather grim otherwise.

Heat the oil in a pan over medium heat and cook the onions for 10 minutes. Stir in the pickled cucumbers and cook for a further 5 minutes. Add the wine, stock, tomatoes, and tomato paste and simmer for 15 minutes or until the pickle slices are soft in the middle but still crunchy on the outside.

Remove from the heat and stir in the dill, reserving a little to garnish. Serve with bread to soak up the delicious juices or with Polenta Dumplings (see page 100).

Serves 2 generously

1 tablespoon vegetable oil or sunflower oil

2 onions, finely sliced

1 lb 5 oz (600 g) mixed pickled
    cucumbers, cut into rounds

Scant ½ cup (100 ml) white wine

1 cup (250 ml) vegetable stock

1 x 14 oz (400 g) can chopped tomatoes

¼ cup (2 oz/60 g) tomato paste

1 bunch of dill, chopped

Ardei umpluți

Stuffed peppers with millet and parsley pesto

In Romania, we are very fond of vegetables stuffed with rice—from peppers and tomatoes to beets and kohlrabi. We use a range of other grains, including millet, which is a good alternative to rice.

Preheat the oven to 350°F (180°C). Cut off the lids of the peppers and remove the seeds. You can rinse them under the tap to get rid of all the tiny seeds. Rub a bit of oil on their skin and sprinkle with salt. Heat a large frying pan on medium heat and fry them briefly on each side, roughly 10 minutes in total. Set aside.

In the same pan, heat a thin layer of oil on medium heat and fry the onions for 10 minutes. Dice the pepper lids and add them to the frying pan along with the carrot, cooking for another 5 minutes. Season with salt, then add the millet and fry for a further 2–3 minutes, stirring gently to combine the grains with the vegetables.

Add 1 cup (250 ml) of the water and cook until it is absorbed. Keep adding water, little by little, until the grains start to soften; this will take 12–15 minutes. The mixture needs to be a fairly tight consistency, but not dry. Set aside.

Meanwhile, make the pesto by combining all the ingredients in a food processor or by using a pestle and mortar. Add the pesto to the millet mixture and stir to combine well. Taste for seasoning—it will most likely need a pinch of salt.

Stuff each pepper with the millet filling and place them in a deep roasting pan. Put any leftover filling in the pan too. Bake for 30 minutes or until the peppers are soft and cooked through.

Serves 4

For the stuffed peppers:
4 large green bell peppers (the
    red ones are too sweet)
Oil, for frying
Salt
2 onions, diced
1 carrot, diced
¾ cup (5 oz/150 g) millet
2 cups (500 ml) water

For the pesto:
1 bunch of parsley
⅓ cup (1 oz/30 g) walnuts
2 tablespoons rapeseed oil or olive oil
⅔ cup (2 oz/60 g) grated Cheddar cheese

Conopidă la cuptor

Cauliflower gratin with sour cream

This cheese-spiked gratin dish is very delicate with the mellow flavor of the cauliflower being lifted by the tangy sour cream. It is really light and refreshing. It can be eaten on its own as a main course, or just as easily served as an appetizer.

Preheat the oven to 400°F (200°C). Grease a deep ceramic dish with butter then sprinkle with the breadcrumbs. Cut the cauliflower into medium-sized florets. Bring a large pan of water to a boil over medium heat and blanch the florets for 6–8 minutes. Drain on paper towels.

 Combine the sour cream, three-quarters of the cheese, eggs, nutmeg, and mustard in a bowl and season with salt and pepper. Place the drained cauliflower into the greased dish, and pour over the sour cream mixture. Sprinkle with the remaining cheese and bake for 25–30 minutes, covering with foil if the top browns too quickly. Serve warm, scattered with sunflower seeds to add crunch.

Serves 4

Butter, for greasing
½ cup (2 oz/60 g) breadcrumbs
1 large cauliflower (around
 2 lb 4 oz/1 kg without leaves)
1½ cups (350 ml) sour cream
4 oz (120 g) Cheddar cheese, grated
2 eggs, beaten
1 teaspoon nutmeg
1 tablespoon mustard
Salt and freshly ground black pepper
½ cup (2 oz/60 g) sunflower
 seeds (optional), to serve

CHAPTER FIVE

Desserts

Traditionally Romanians don't eat dessert every day, but we do love to bake, and layered cakes are the pride and glory of any household. In the countryside, we love a good *plăcintă*—stuffed layered breads with a sweet filling of stewed fruits or cheese curds with raisins. The cities have *prăjitură* and *tort*, which can be anything from a clafoutis-style dessert to a luscious, chocolate-layered cake.

We bake for special occasions and religious celebrations and to mark moments of happiness, togetherness, merry-making, and fun. When eating out, choosing something from the dessert menu is a must, even if we only order crêpes with cherry preserves. Patisserie shops, *cofetării*, are dotted around cities and towns, displaying anything from baklavas and *cataifs* to Savarin cakes, *choux-à-la-crème* cream puffs, and chocolate mousses. It is a seductive, fairytale world of the old Byzantium meeting the western sweet cuisines of Austria and France.

Our love affair with layered cakes, coffee houses, *cafenele*, and patisserie shops started during the Austrian Empire and Habsburg rule, when the empire itself was enjoying a period of culinary sophistication. This is probably the sweetest thing that happened to us under the circumstances.

Cozonac

Walnut and rum celebration bread

Makes 2 loaves

This is the traditional Romanian celebration bread for Easter and Christmas—richer than a brioche and loaded with a rum-spiked walnut filling. My contribution as kitchen helper was to hold down the kneading bowl while my mom lifted the dough in the air, and slapped it right back down in the middle. This was her technique for incorporating the butter. In spring *cozonac* is baked on the last Thursday before Easter Sunday, creating wonderful aromas in every house and bakery, making your day feel glorious as you stroll through the alleys.

To make the *maia*, combine all of the ingredients in a bowl, cover, and set aside in a warm place for 25 minutes or until doubled in size.

To make the dough, dissolve the yeast in the milk. In a separate bowl, combine the egg yolks with the salt, then add the sugar and rum. Pour the egg mixture over the *maia* and add the milk and yeast, then gradually add the flour, citrus zests, and vanilla extract. Transfer to the bowl of an electric mixer fitted with a dough hook. Knead for about 10 minutes or until the dough is soft and comes away from the sides of the bowl. Add the butter, a little at a time, kneading after each addition until well incorporated. (I prefer to do this by hand as it is more gentle on the dough, and you can feel the mixture becoming silky and elastic—an indication that the butter has been well incorporated.) Leave to rise in a warm place (over 70°F/21°C) for 1½–2 hours.

To make the filling, fold all of the remaining ingredients into the whisked egg whites and set aside.

If the dough is too soft to handle after rising, knock the air out of it and refrigerate for 30 minutes. Use some oil to grease a work surface, turn out the dough, and divide in four. Using your fingertips, stretch one of the pieces of dough into a rectangle about 16 by 12 inch (40 by 30 cm). With the long side parallel to you, spread a fourth of the filling evenly onto the dough and roll it into a log. Repeat the process with the remaining dough.

Grease two 9 by 5 inch (23 by 13 cm) loaf pans. Place one log over another to form an X shape. Twist the logs of dough together, starting with one side of the X, then repeat with the other side. Place the twisted dough into the pan, doubling over itself to make it fit. Repeat the process with the remaining two pieces of dough, then cover with a damp dish towel. Leave to proof in a warm place for at least 1 hour.

Preheat the oven to 375°F (190°C). Glaze the bread very gently with the egg wash and bake for 25 minutes. Lower the heat to 350°F (180°C) and bake for a further 20 minutes, covering with foil if the top browns too quickly. Cool the *cozonac* upside-down on a wire rack, to prevent the bottom from becoming soggy. Serve sliced with a glass of hot milk.

For the *maia* (pre-ferment):
¼ cup (1 oz/30 g) all-purpose flour
¼ cup (60 ml) tepid milk
1 teaspoon sugar
2 teaspoons (¼ oz/7 g) active dry yeast

For the dough:
1½ tablespoons (½ oz/15 g) active dry yeast
½ cup (120 ml) tepid milk
6 egg yolks
½ teaspoon salt
½ cup (3½ oz/100 g) sugar
2 tablespoons rum
3½ cups (1 lb/450 g) all-purpose flour
Zest of 1 orange
Zest of 1 lemon
1 tablespoon vanilla extract
7 tablespoons (3½ oz/100 g) butter, melted
Vegetable oil or sunflower oil, for greasing

For the filling:
2 egg whites, whisked to very soft peaks
2 cups (7 oz/200 g) walnuts, ground
3 tablespoons instant coffee
¼ cup (¾ oz/20 g) cocoa powder
2 tablespoons rum
¾ cup (5 oz/150 g) sugar

For the glaze:
1 egg yolk, whisked with 1 tablespoon milk

Papanași

Ricotta doughnuts
served with sour cherry jam and crème fraîche

The ultimate comfort dessert—exuberant and rustic, *papanași* are the great big ending to any Romanian meal. We say that they are a bit like life: sweet, sour, round, and imperfect. The doughnuts must be light and not too sweet, since most of the sweetness comes from the jam. Be generous with the jam and crème fraîche. It's all a balancing act, but in the end you add as much of each topping as you wish. I love the sour cherry jam, so I'm biased. In the summer, I replace the crème fraîche with a dollop of ice cream.

Makes 10–12

For the doughnuts:
1¼ cups (10½ oz/300 g) fresh
     ricotta (see page 210)
Scant ½ cup (3½ oz/100 g) plain
     yogurt
1 egg
2 tablespoons sugar
2 teaspoons vanilla extract
Salt
2 cups (9 oz/250 g) all-purpose
     flour, plus extra for flouring
1 teaspoon baking powder
Zest of 1 orange

For frying:
Scant ½ cup (100 ml) vegetable
     oil or sunflower oil

To serve:
⅓ cup (2½ oz/75 g) crème fraîche
¼ cup (2½ oz/75 g) sour cherry jam
Confectioners' sugar, for dusting

To make the doughnuts, mix together the ricotta, yogurt, egg, sugar, vanilla extract, and a pinch of salt. Add the flour, baking powder, and orange zest, mixing until you see the dough coming together and away from the sides of the bowl. It will be a bit sticky, but refrigerate for 30 minutes to make it easier to work with. Though the dough will remain sticky throughout the whole process—it's what gives the doughnuts their fluffiness and lightness.

Flour your hands and roll the dough into 20–24 balls. Half of the balls should be 2 inches in diameter (2 oz/60 g), the other half ½ inch in diameter (½ oz/15 g). These will be your *papanași* pairs. Take one larger ball and use the handle of a wooden spoon to make a hole in the center, then rotate the spoon with a stirring action to create a doughnut ring. Repeat with the remaining larger balls. Leave the smaller balls as they are—they will go on top of the larger ones.

Heat the oil in a deep pan (or a fryer) until piping hot, then reduce the heat to medium. If you have a thermometer, the temperature should be 350°F (180°C). Working quickly, fry both the rings and balls for 2–3 minutes. They will get quite dark, but this is what you are looking for. Set aside to drain on paper towels.

To serve, place the doughnut rings on a plate and cover each with a generous dollop of crème fraîche, then top with a spoonful of jam. Add a small doughnut ball on top of each ring and dust with confectioners' sugar. Serve warm and enjoy!

Doboş Tort

Seven layer Hungarian cake

This is an extravagant cake of rich chocolate buttercream studded with roasted walnuts and finished with a bitter-sweet caramel topping. We owe its popularity to the Austro-Hungarian empire, so much so that its bane even made it into the communist cooking books where dishes that sounded foreign were usually renamed. For years I had a simplified version of it for my birthday, but here I want to make it in all its glory.

To make the sponge cake, preheat the oven to 400°F (200°C). Grease and line the cake pans with parchment paper—if you don't have seven, bake the mixture in batches. Whisk the eggs and sugar together until pale and fluffy. Fold in the butter and sift in the flour, combining well. Spoon about ½ cup (3½ oz/100 g) of the mixture into each pan and bake for 10–12 minutes, or until golden. Remove from the pans and carefully peel away the parchment paper while the cakes are still warm. Stack all seven one on top of the other, cover with a dish towel so they retain as much moisture as possible, and set aside.

To make the buttercream, beat the butter with the sugar until creamy, then add the eggs one by one (if the mixture splits, don't panic—it will come back together once the chocolate is added). Add the instant coffee and chocolate, stir to combine, and refrigerate for 30 minutes.

To make the top layer, place one of the 7 sponge cake layers on a cooling rack with a plate underneath, ready to pour the caramel over. Pass the blade of a long carving knife through butter and set aside.

To make the caramel, heat the sugar with the water in a small pan over medium heat until the sugar darkens and caramelizes. This is a very quick process, so don't take your eyes off the pan! Pour the caramel over the prepared sponge cake layer and down the sides as evenly as possible. It will solidify very quickly, so work fast. Take the knife and quickly cut the caramel-covered layer into 8 triangles. You might need to pass the knife edge through butter a few times.

To assemble, spread ⅓ cup (3½ oz/100 g) of the buttercream over each of the six sponge cake layers, then use the remaining buttercream to cover the sides and top—you will only need a thin layer. Now press the walnuts around the sides, leaving the top bare. Arrange the 8 caramel triangles on the top and refrigerate overnight.

Serves 8

7 x 7 inch (18 cm) round cake pans
Butter, for greasing and top layer

For the sponge cake:
7 eggs
¾ cup (5 oz/150 g) sugar
6 tablespoons (3 oz/80 g) butter,
    melted and cooled
1¼ cup (5 oz/150 g) all-purpose flour

For the buttercream:
3 sticks (12 oz/350 g) butter, softened
Generous 1 cup (8 oz/225 g)
    confectioners' sugar
2 eggs, at room temperature
2 tablespoons instant coffee
8 oz (225 g) dark chocolate, melted

For the caramel:
½ cup (3½ oz/100 g) sugar
1 tablespoon water

To assemble:
1 cup (3½ oz/100 g) walnuts,
    finely chopped

Învârtită

Apple and blueberry swirl pie

How wonderful to name a cake after a traditional Romanian dance, *învârtită*. Couples put their arms on each others shoulders and spin around elegantly, women swirling their beautiful pleated skirts and marking the pace with a quick stomp. It is part of village life at celebrations or on Sundays after church, when people love to play music, dance, and eat good food. This pie can be made with a savory or sweet filling, but I am biased towards the fruity one— juicy and just a bit indulgent.

Serves 6

For the dough:

2 cups (9 oz/250 g) all-purpose
    flour, plus extra for dusting
2 teaspoons vegetable oil or sunflower
    oil, plus extra for greasing
1 egg
Scant ½ cup (100 ml) milk

For the filling:

1 large apple, peeled, cored, and diced
2 tablespoons sugar
Splash of lemon juice
1 teaspoon cinnamon

To assemble:

4 tablespoons (2½ oz/60 g) butter, melted
¾ cup (2½ oz/75 g) ground almonds
¾ cup (3½ oz/100 g) blueberries

For the syrup:

¼ cup (2 oz/60 g) sugar
¼ cup (60 ml) water

To make the dough, mix all the ingredients together and knead for about 10 minutes. The whole process of making this pie is quite tactile, so I like to knead the dough by hand and feel its texture turning smooth and springy. Refrigerate the dough while you make the filling.

To make the filling, put the apple, sugar, and lemon juice into a pan over low heat and cook gently until the apple is soft but not mashed. Add the cinnamon and set aside to cool.

Preheat the oven to 400°F (200°C). Grease and line a 9 inch (23 cm) round cake pan or springform pan.

Place a clean dish towel measuring about 25 by 20 inches (65 by 50 cm) on a work surface, with one of the long edges closest to you. Dust the dish towel generously with flour and place the dough in the center. Using a floured rolling pin, roll the dough until it is very thin, about ⅛ inch (3 mm) thick, and covers the dish towel (you may need to use your fingers to stretch it to the edges).

Brush the dough with 2 tablespoons of the melted butter, then evenly sprinkle over the ground almonds. Spread the apple filling onto the dough, then dot with the blueberries. Grab the edge of the dish towel and use it to roll the pastry gently away from you into a log, then wrap the log into a tight coil. Brush the coil lightly with the remaining melted butter, place in the prepared pan, and bake for 30 minutes.

To make the syrup, place the sugar and water in a pan over medium heat and bring to a boil, then leave to simmer for 5 minutes.

Remove the pie from the oven, brush all over with the syrup, then bake for a further 5 minutes.

Leave to cool slightly, but serve warm.

Pască

Brioche baked cheesecake

This cheesecake is our equivalent of eating chocolate eggs for Easter and it's baked only for this occasion. Baskets of food, with *Cozonac* (see page 147), painted eggs, and *pască* are lined up at church on the eve of Easter Sunday for the priest's blessing during the sunrise service. They are then taken home and shared with loved ones in a delicious feast, ending the fasting period. For me, breathing in the scent of this cake is a moment of happiness. Buttery and sweet, it is a powerful reminder of the meaning of Easter, when we rejoice and indulge in celebrations.

To make the brioche dough, put the flour, milk, yeast, and sugar into the bowl of an electric mixer fitted with a dough hook. Mix on medium speed until well combined, then add the eggs one by one and mix again. When the dough starts to come away from the sides of the bowl, start adding the butter, dice by dice, ensuring that each addition is well incorporated. Cover and leave to rise in a warm place (over 70°F/21°C) for 1½–2 hours. It will be too soft to work with at this stage—refrigerate for 2–3 hours or overnight and it will be ready to roll.

To make the filling, thoroughly combine all the ingredients together to form a smooth mixture.

Divide the dough in two. Line a baking sheet with parchment paper and grease a 10 inch (25 cm) cake ring or springform pan with its base removed. Using a rolling pin, roll half of the dough into a circle slightly larger than the ring or pan, and place it onto the baking sheet. Place the ring or pan on top of the pastry circle (you will trim the excess later).

Divide the remaining half of the dough in two. Roll into two ropes, measuring about 34 inches (87 cm) long. Loosely twist the dough ropes together, leaving room for the dough to expand. Place inside the ring or pan, creating a beautiful twisted border around the sides.

Preheat the oven to 375°F (190°C). Brush the twisted border with the egg wash, then pour the filling inside the border. Scatter the orange zest on top and dot with the diced butter.

Bake for 25–30 minutes until the filling is soft and wobbly in the middle. If the dough becomes too dark during baking, cover with foil. Cool on a wire rack before trimming any excess dough outside the cake ring. Remove the cake ring by running a knife along its edge to loosen it, then lift away. If using a springform pan, simply open it to release from the cake.

Serve for dessert or as a treat for breakfast. If you have any raisins left, scatter them on top.

Serves 6

For the brioche:

2½ cups (10½ oz/300 g) white bread flour

2 tablespoons milk, at room temperature

2 teaspoons (¼ oz/7 g) active dry yeast

1 tablespoon sugar

3 eggs

10 tablespoons (5 oz/150 g) butter, diced and softened, plus extra for greasing

For the filling:

Generous ¾ cup (7 oz/200 g) fresh ricotta (see page 210) or ½ cup (3½ oz/100 g) store-bought ricotta mixed with ½ cup (3½ oz/100 g) crème fraîche

3 egg yolks

3 tablespoons sugar

½ cup (3½ oz/100 g) raisins

1 tablespoon orange liqueur or rum (optional)

1 teaspoon vanilla extract

For baking:

1 egg yolk, mixed with 1 teaspoon milk

Zest of 1 orange

1 tablespoon butter, diced

Tort de mere

Caramelized apple cake

This is a cake for the beginning of autumn, when chilly nights make us crave comforting baked apples with caramel sauce. It is traditionally served with whipped cream, to which I like to add a little brandy, but you may wish to try it with Cider Ice Cream (see page 211) for its refreshing acidity and flavor. However, the cake is perfect on its own and although it's best the following day, it usually doesn't last that long.

To prepare the apples, cut away the tops and scoop out the core, then cut the bottoms to create a flat base. Add a tablespoon of jam into each apple. Preheat the oven to 400°F (200°C).

To make the caramel sauce, melt the sugar and butter together in a 9 inch (23 cm) round, 3 inch (8 cm) deep ovenproof pan over medium heat. Cook until the sugar is dark brown in color, stirring continuously. Add the apples, jam-side up, transfer to the oven, and bake for 20 minutes.

Meanwhile, make the batter: whisk the eggs with the sugar until pale, then pour in the butter. Add the ground almonds and a pinch of salt, and mix well. Add the remaining ingredients and whisk to combine.

Remove the pan from the oven and pour the batter around the apples. Return the pan to the oven and bake for 10 minutes, then reduce the heat to 350°F (180°C) and bake for a further 20 minutes.

Remove from the oven and very carefully run a knife all around the edge. Rest for 5 minutes, then put a plate on top of the pan and carefully, but quickly, turn it upside-down to reveal the cake. Set aside to cool completely before serving with Cider Ice Cream or Brandy Chantilly Cream.

Serves 6

For the apples:
5 medium apples
5 tablespoons (3½ oz/100 g) jam
    (your favorite flavor)

For the caramel sauce:
Generous ½ cup (4 oz/120 g) sugar
3 tablespoons (1½ oz/40 g) butter

For the batter:
4 eggs
¾ cup (5 oz/150 g) sugar
8 tablespoons (4 oz/120 g) butter,
    melted and cooled to lukewarm
1½ cups (5 oz/150 g) ground almonds
Salt
Zest of 1 lemon
1 tablespoon vanilla extract
1 teaspoon baking powder

To serve:
Cider ice cream (see page 211)
Brandy chantilly cream (see page 211)

Salam de biscuiți

Aunt Geta's chocolate "salami"

A chocolate salami is one of the easiest no-bake treats to make, and despite the name, doesn't require any chocolate. In communist times, chocolate was a rarity—we probably only had it once a year, and it was imported from China. So to have this finger-licking chocolate flavor was a joyous occasion, and I owe this recipe to my aunt Geta. She makes the best salami ever (and a toffee vodka to blow your socks off!), and her trick for the salami is to use halva, which in Romania is made of sunflower seeds.

Serves 10–12

3 tablespoons raisins

3 tablespoons rum

7 oz (200 g) digestive cookies or graham crackers, crushed

1 cup (3½ oz/100 g) walnuts, roasted and chopped

⅓ cup (80 ml) water

¼ cup (2 oz/60 g) sugar

Scant ½ cup (1 oz/30 g) cocoa powder

1 tablespoon orange marmalade

1 tablespoon vanilla extract

Zest of 1 orange

½ cup (3½ oz/100 g) vanilla halva, roughly chopped

Confectioners' sugar or shredded coconut, to serve

Soak the raisins in the rum for 15–20 minutes while you crush the cookies and roast and chop the walnuts.

Gently bring the water to a boil in a pan over low heat, pour in the sugar, and stir to dissolve. Remove from the heat and add the cocoa powder, combining well.

Drain the raisins, discarding the rum. In a bowl, mix the raisins with the crushed cookies, walnuts, marmalade, vanilla extract, and orange zest. Add the cooled sugar mixture and combine well. Add the halva at the last minute. Transfer the mixture onto a layer of plastic wrap and shape it into a log. Refrigerate overnight. When you are ready to serve, remove the salami from the plastic wrap and roll it in confectioners' sugar or shredded coconut before cutting into slices to serve.

Chisăliță de prune cu mămăligă

Stewed plums with honey polenta "porridge"

This dish is usually served poured over a piece of bread or polenta. It is somewhere between a stew and a soup, and the exact consistency depends on regional interpretations. In some parts of the country the stewed plums are strained then thickened with polenta. My Transylvanian grandmother used to serve this as a lunch and dessert in one.

Bring the plums and water to a boil over medium heat then simmer until the fruit is soft and pulpy, stirring occasionally. Set aside to cool slightly. The mixture should be the consistency of a thin compote.

Bring the milk and honey to a boil in a separate pan over medium heat then turn the heat down to low. Add the polenta and whisk thoroughly until it absorbs the liquid and becomes soft and creamy.

Divide the polenta into two bowls and pour over a little of the plum mixture. Drizzle with honey and sprinkle over a little cinnamon, if desired.

Serves 2

14 oz (400 g) plums, pitted and sliced
4 cups (1 liter) water
Scant 1 cup (200 ml) milk
2 tablespoons liquid honey,
    plus extra to serve
½ cup (2 oz/60 g) coarse polenta
Cinnamon, to serve (optional)

Chec

Summer fruit marble cake

The name actually comes from the English "cake" and it is one of the most popular and versatile bakes in Romania. When it comes to flavors, there are no rules—you can use any of your favorite ones, combined or not, then serve it glazed, topped with fresh fruit or whipped cream, or just plain. It is so popular that you can even find savory versions! It is an incredibly light cake, and very refreshing with its bounty of summer fruits.

To make the syrup, bring the fruit and sugar to a boil in a deep pan, then reduce the heat and simmer for 10–12 minutes, or until soft and sticky. While still warm, pass through a sieve to squeeze out all of that wonderful juice—you should now have around ¼ cup (60 ml) of dense, fruity syrup.

To make the cake, whisk the egg whites until they form soft peaks, then add the sugar gradually and whisk to a stiff meringue-like consistency. Combine the egg yolks with the oil, then fold into the egg whites and sugar. Sift in the flour with the baking powder, combining well. Divide the mixture into two separate bowls. Fold the vanilla extract into one bowl and the fruit syrup into the other.

Preheat the oven to 350°F (180°C). Grease and line a 9 by 5 inch (23 by 13 cm) loaf pan, then starting in the center, drop in 2 tablespoons of the vanilla batter followed by 2 tablespoons of the fruit batter. Continue alternating with the remaining batter—it will soon spread to fill the pan on its own. The mixture should come two-thirds up the sides of the pan.

Bake for 35–40 minutes or until a wooden skewer comes out clean. Leave to rest in the pan for 10 minutes, then turn out and leave to cool. Dust with confectioners' sugar and serve with fruit.

Serves 8–10

For the syrup:
7 oz (200 g) summer fruits
   (fresh or frozen)
3 tablespoons sugar

For the cake:
4 eggs, separated
¾ cup (5 oz/150 g) sugar
2 tablespoons olive oil, plus
   extra for greasing
1¼ cup (5 oz/150 g) all-purpose flour
1 teaspoon baking powder
1 tablespoon vanilla extract

To serve:
Confectioners' sugar, for dusting
Fresh or poached fruit

Cremşnit

Vanilla custard slice

To me, this dessert has the resonance of the elegant world of our royal family. Queen Marie of Romania was the granddaughter of Queen Victoria and she was born in Kent, England. One of their family homes outside Bucharest was the marvelous Peleş Castle, built in a flamboyant Renaissance-revival style. I can imagine this dessert being served there after a long dinner due to its light yet velvety texture, just enough to satisfy a sweet tooth.

Preheat the oven to 400°F (200°C) and line 2 baking sheets with parchment paper. If using homemade pastry, divide the dough in two. Roll both halves to 12 by 14 inch (30 by 35 cm) rectangles around ¼ inch (5 mm) thick. Place each pastry rectangle, or puff-pastry sheet, on a baking sheet and bake for 20–25 minutes until golden and crispy. While still warm, trim one pastry rectangle to the size of the rectangular dish you will use to assemble the cake (mine was 9 by 11 inches/23 by 28 cm). Reserve the trimmings and second pastry rectangle for the topping.

To make the vanilla cream, mix the egg yolks with the sugar in a bowl, then add the flour and cornstarch. In a pan over medium heat, heat the milk with the vanilla extract. Gradually add the warm milk to the bowl with the eggs, stirring continuously. Return the mixture to the pan, bring to a simmer, and whisk until thickened. Remove from the heat and leave to cool for 15 minutes, then add the butter, combining well. Set aside to cool completely.

To make the whipped cream, whisk the cream with the confectioners' sugar until soft peaks form, then stir in the vanilla extract and orange liqueur, if using. Be careful not to over whip—it's easily done. Set aside.

To assemble the cake, line a rectangular baking dish with plastic wrap, allowing it to overhang on each side. Place the trimmed pastry layer into the dish, spread the vanilla cream on top, then add the whipped cream. Cover with the overhanging plastic wrap and place in the fridge overnight. When you are ready to serve, crumble over the reserved pastry rectangle and trimmings. Cut into rectangular slices and dust with confectioners' sugar.

Serves 8–10

For the pastry:
1 quantity of pastry dough (see page 65), or 2 x 11½ oz (320 g) store-bought puff pastry sheets

For the vanilla cream:
6 egg yolks
Generous ½ cup (4 oz/120 g) sugar
¼ cup (1 oz/30 g) all-purpose flour
Scant ¼ cup (1 oz/30 g) cornstarch
2 cups (500 ml) milk
1 tablespoon vanilla extract
4 tablespoons (2 oz/60 g) unsalted butter, diced

For the whipped cream:
1 cup (250 ml) heavy whipping cream
2 tablespoons confectioners' sugar, plus extra for dusting
1 teaspoon vanilla extract
¼ cup (60 ml) orange liqueur (optional)

Prăjitură cu ciocolată

Chocolate cream cakes

These may look complicated, but they are actually pretty straightforward to make. They were initially called Moors' Heads or *Indiene*, the connection being an exotic juggling act which inspired a pastry chef and a Hungarian theater director to use them as incentives for selling tickets. Today they are more commonly known as chocolate kisses, buns, or cream cakes.

Preheat the oven to 350°F (180°C). Line a baking sheet with parchment paper and use a pencil to draw sixteen 3 inch (8 cm) circles onto the paper.

To make the sponge cake discs, whisk the egg whites until they form soft peaks, then add the sugar and cream of tartar, whisking to the consistency of stiff meringue. Add the egg yolks and lemon juice and zest, sift in the flour, and fold gently until well incorporated. Pipe or spoon equal quantities of the mixture into each drawn circle, if possible forming a slight dome shape. Bake for 15 minutes, or until firm and golden in color, then cool on a wire rack.

To make the filling, whisk the cream with the confectioners' sugar until thick, then gently add the melted chocolate, combining well. Transfer to a pastry bag and refrigerate to firm up.

To make the syrup, bring the water and sugar to a boil in a pan over medium heat. Simmer for 8–10 minutes until slightly reduced. Remove from the heat and stir in the rum or brandy. Leave to cool.

To assemble, take half the sponge cake discs and dip the tops, one by one, into the chocolate glaze, then set aside—the chocolate doesn't have to be even around the edges. Take the unglazed discs and brush them with a little of the rum syrup, then pipe the chocolate cream filling on top. Place the glazed discs on top of the filling, then spoon over or pipe a little of the whipped cream onto each one. Dust with cocoa powder, if desired. Serve on the day of making.

Makes 8

For the sponge cake discs:
3 eggs, separated
¼ cup (2 oz/60 g) sugar
1 teaspoon cream of tartar
Juice and zest of 1 lemon
⅔ cup (2½ oz/75 g) all-purpose flour

For the filling:
⅔ cup (150 ml) heavy cream,
    at room temperature
¼ cup (1 oz/30 g) confectioners' sugar
4½ oz (125 g) dark chocolate, melted

For the syrup:
Scant ½ cup (100 ml) water
½ cup (3½ oz/100 g) sugar
¼ cup (60 ml) rum or brandy

For the chocolate glaze:
3½ oz (100 g) milk chocolate, melted

To assemble:
Scant 1 cup (200 ml) heavy
    whipping cream, whipped
Cocoa powder (optional)

Cataif

Shredded filo nests with walnuts and whipped cream

Makes 12

For the walnut filling:
¾ cup (2½ oz/75 g) walnuts,
    chopped or ground
1 tablespoon (½ oz/15 g) butter,
    melted, plus extra for greasing
Zest of 1 lemon
2 teaspoons vanilla extract
Salt

For the rolls:
12 oz (350 g) *kataifi* pastry (shredded
    filo dough)
14 tablespoons (7 oz/200 g) butter,
    melted

For the syrup:
1¼ cup (9 oz/250 g) sugar
Scant ½ cup (100 ml) water
Juice of 2 oranges

To serve:
Scant ½ cup (100 ml) heavy
    whipping cream, whipped
Zest of 1 orange

Entering a *cofetărie* pastry shop in Bucharest is really a historical trip through baking and cakes. In the window you will see Greek and Turkish baklavas, *cataifs*, filo pies, and sherbets, alongside French-influenced buttercream layer cakes, chocolate mousses, and fruit tarts. In the late 19th century, Romania swapped its caftans for the crinolines, and began its own journey in cake-making and patisserie. This *cataif* is the ultimate nutty extravagance, where sticky walnuts are paired with thin, crunchy shreds of *kataifi* pastry, which can be found in middle-eastern shops or bought online, and served with dollops of whipped cream on top.

Preheat the oven to 400°F (200°C) and grease a deep baking pan. To make the filling, pulse all the ingredients together, along with a pinch of salt, in a food processor and set aside.

To make the rolls, work the *kataifi* pastry by tearing it apart gently, strand by strand, until fluffed-up. Take a handful of pastry and brush it generously with the melted butter. Place a tablespoon or 2 of the walnut filling in the middle, and roll it like a cigar. Put the roll into the pan and repeat with the remaining pastry and filling. Brush the tops of the rolls with the remaining melted butter. Bake for 15–20 minutes or until crispy and dark golden.

Meanwhile, make the syrup by bringing all of the ingredients to a boil in a small pan over medium heat.

Pour the syrup over the hot *cataif* and set aside to cool, allowing the syrup to be totally absorbed. Serve topped with whipped cream and a sprinkling of orange zest.

Prăjitura cu caise

Apricot yogurt cake

Romanians love to bake with fruit, and we are blessed with plenty of it. This cake is very easy to make and can be made with apricots, cherries, peaches, blueberries, or pears to create a multitude of versions and colors. The slightly sticky yogurt cake is the perfect accompaniment to the delicate flavor of the apricots. It's just the thing you need on a summer evening, with a scoop of ice cream or a little sprinkle of fresh tarragon—the anise flavor of the tarragon contrasting so well with the sweetness of the apricots.

Serves 6

3 eggs, separated

¾ cup (5 oz/150 g) sugar

¼ cup (60 ml) olive oil or canola oil, plus extra for greasing

¼ cup (2 oz/60 g) plain yogurt

1 teaspoon vanilla extract

Salt

1¼ cups (5 oz/150 g) all-purpose flour

1 teaspoon baking powder

4–5 fresh apricots, halved

Confectioners' sugar, for dusting

Preheat the oven to 350°F (180°C). Grease and line a deep 11 by 9 inch (30 by 23 cm) baking pan. Whisk the egg whites until they form soft peaks and set aside. Beat the egg yolks with the sugar, then add the oil, yogurt, vanilla extract, and a pinch of salt, stirring well to emulsify. Add the flour and baking powder then gently fold in the egg whites.

Pour the cake batter into the pan, then arrange the apricot halves on top, cut-side up. Bake for 30 minutes or until the cake is firm to the touch. Leave to cool in the pan, then dust with confectioners' sugar and cut into long rectangular slices to serve.

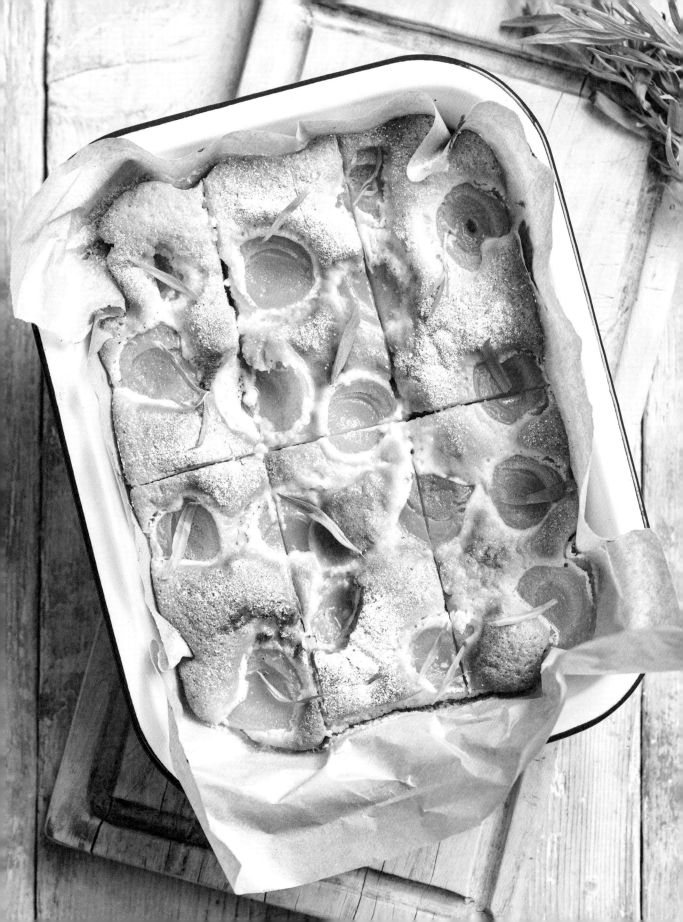

Şodou cu tăiţei şi piersici

Noodle pudding with grilled peaches

This pudding brings back memories of my mom making it for me, and waiting impatiently next to the stove to eat it straight from the pan. She used condensed milk instead of cream for its caramelized flavor. When this wasn't available, she would add egg yolks to the mixture right after taking the pan off the heat, to give a thicker, silky consistency. This basic mixture of milk with egg is called şodou—from the French *chaud-d'oeuf*, meaning "warm egg"—and is often served with fruits or coffee.

To make the noodles, mix together the eggs with the flour to form a dough. If it has a crumbly texture, add 1 tablespoon of water and mix again, adding more water if necessary. Knead by hand for 8–10 minutes, then place an upturned bowl over the dough and leave to rest for 15 minutes.

Flour a work surface and roll the dough into a large circle about ⅛ inch (3 mm) thick, or as thin as you can. Sprinkle with a little flour and leave to dry for 30 minutes or more, depending on how dry your kitchen is. Roll the circle into a loose log and slice thinly. Leave the noodles to dry on a clean dish towel for a further 10 minutes.

Meanwhile, preheat the oven to 400°F (200°C), and put the peach halves onto a baking sheet. Combine the honey with the cinnamon, drizzle over the peaches, and roast for 15 minutes. Set aside in a bowl.

To make the pudding, put the milk and cream in a pan over low heat and slowly bring to a boil. Add the honey, turn the heat down to low, and add the noodles. Simmer gently for 10 minutes—the pudding needs to be quite thick.

Remove the pan from the heat, add the vanilla extract, and wait for 5 minutes. Combine a little of the liquid pudding mixture with the egg yolk, mixing well and bringing it up to the same temperature as the pan, then pour the egg yolk mixture over the noodles, stirring continuously for a couple of minutes until the mixture has a light golden glow and is thickened.

Transfer to serving bowls, then add the grilled peaches and spoon over a little of their roasting sauce.

Serves 4

For the noodles:
2 eggs, beaten
Scant 1½ cups (6 oz/175 g) all-purpose
    flour, plus extra for flouring

For the peaches:
4 ripe peaches, halved
1 tablespoon liquid honey
1 teaspoon cinnamon

For the pudding:
1¾ cups (400 ml) milk
Scant ½ cup (100 ml) heavy cream
3 tablespoons liquid honey
1 teaspoon vanilla extract
1 egg yolk

Albiniṭa

Little honey bee cake

This gorgeous layer cake will change the way you view semolina forever. Tucked between layers of honey sponge cake sits a sumptuous semolina filling paired with tangy rosehip jam. Romanians are very fond of their honey, which is usually made from the blossom of linden or acacia trees, with a very delicate scent of wild flowers. This cake is a marvelous celebration of some of our beloved Romanian ingredients.

Serves 8

For the sponge cake:
¼ cup (3 oz/85 g) honey
⅓ cup (2½ oz/75 g) sugar
3 tablespoons (1½ oz/40 g) butter
1 egg
1 tablespoon vanilla extract
Zest of 1 lemon
1 tablespoon cold milk
2½ cups (10½ oz/300 g) all-purpose flour
½ teaspoon baking powder

For the semolina filling:
2 cups (450 ml) milk
3½ tablespoons honey
Scant 1 cup (5 oz/150 g) semolina
4 teaspoons vanilla extract
Pinch of salt
14 tablespoons (7 oz/200 g)
    butter, diced and softened
Zest of 1 lemon

For the jam layer:
¾ cup (9 oz/250 g) rosehip jam
    or another tangy flavor

To serve:
Confectioners' sugar, for dusting

To make the sponge cake, melt together the honey, sugar, and butter in a small saucepan. Bring to a simmer, then set aside to cool. In a bowl, mix together the egg, vanilla extract, lemon zest, milk, and cooled honey mixture. Sift in the flour and baking powder, and briefly knead to form a dough. Refrigerate for 30 minutes while you make the filling.

To make the semolina filling, bring the milk and honey to a boil in a pan. Turn the heat down and gradually add the semolina, stirring well to avoid any lumps forming. Add the vanilla extract and salt and set aside to cool. When the filling reaches room temperature, add the butter and lemon zest and combine until very well incorporated.

Preheat the oven to 400°F (200°C) and line 2 baking sheets with parchment paper. Remove the dough from the fridge and divide into 4 even-sized balls. Roll each ball into a 9 inch (22 cm) circle. Transfer to the baking sheets, prick with a fork, and bake for 8–9 minutes or until firm to the touch and golden in color. While still warm, trim each to an 8 inch (20 cm) circle, using a plate or cake pan as your guide. Stack the sponge cake layers on a plate and cover with a dish towel to retain as much moisture as possible. Set aside to cool.

Line an 8 inch (20 cm) springform pan with plastic wrap. Place a sponge-cake layer into the pan, then spread over half of the semolina filling. Add a second sponge-cake layer and press down gently. Spread over a layer of jam, then add a third sponge-cake layer. Spread over the remaining semolina filling, then place the last sponge-cake layer on top. Refrigerate overnight. When you are ready to serve, carefully remove the cake from the pan, peel away the plastic wrap, and dust with confectioners' sugar.

Tort de înghețată cassata

Cassata-style ice cream cake

Cassata is the famous Sicilian cake made with candied fruit and a ricotta filling, that somehow landed in Romania as an ice cream cake. Layers of velvety ice cream and cherry jam are covered by a thin dark chocolate glaze, turning this cake into one of the most decadent desserts in Bucharest. I have dared to change it here a little so that you don't need an ice cream machine to make it, and instead serve it with fresh cherries. It is an impressive centerpiece, and all you need is a little patience over a few hours while the ice cream layers are setting. You can make this a few days in advance.

To make the pistachio paste, pulse all of ingredients in a food processor or grind with a mortar and pestle until they come together to form a paste.

To make the chocolate base, pulse the ingredients in a food processor until combined.

To make the ice cream, whip the cream to soft peaks. In a separate bowl, combine the condensed milk with the ricotta until smooth, then fold in the whipped cream. Divide the mixture evenly between two bowls. Add the pistachio paste to the first bowl and the cherries and vanilla extract to the second bowl, stirring both to combine well.

Line an 8 inch (20 cm) springform cake pan with plastic wrap. Press the chocolate mixture into the pan to create an even base.

Pour the pistachio ice cream mixture over the base and level gently. Place the pan in the freezer. Refrigerate the cherry ice cream mixture. The pistachio ice cream will set in around 2 hours—it doesn't have to be rock hard, just firm enough to support the second layer.

Once set, add the cherry ice cream mixture to the cake pan and return to the freezer overnight to set, or until needed.

Remove the cake from the pan a few minutes before serving. Decorate with the fresh cherries and spoonfuls of their sauce.

Serves 8

For the pistachio paste:

¾ cup (3½ oz/100 g) shelled pistachios

2 tablespoons canola oil

1 tablespoon ground almonds

½ teaspoon almond extract

2 tablespoons Marsala wine or rum

For the chocolate base:

7 oz (200 g) digestive cookies
    or graham crackers

4 tablespoons (2 oz/60 g) butter, melted

3 tablespoons cocoa powder

For the ice cream:

2¼ cups (500 ml) heavy cream

1¾ cups (400 ml) condensed milk

Generous ¾ cup (7 oz/200 g) fresh
    ricotta (see page 210)

1 quantity pistachio paste (see above)

1 cup (5 oz/150 g) fresh cherries,
    pitted and halved

2 tablespoons vanilla extract

To decorate:

½ cup (2 oz/60 g) fresh cherries,
    pitted, halved, and lightly stewed
    with 2 tablespoons sugar

Cornulețe cu gem

Mini crescent rolls with jam or Turkish delight

These little crescent rolls are very addictive, and go so well with a cup of coffee or tea. They are something that we would take to the neighbors when passing by to say hello. We have a custom in Romania not to visit someone empty-handed, and we usually bring homemade treats with us. The host would have to reciprocate and never return the plate empty, even if all they have is fruit, freshly baked bread, or shelled walnuts. It was hard for me to decide between the two fillings so I'm giving you both versions, equally popular at home: jam and Turkish delight.

Makes 24

For the dough:

2¾ cups (12 oz/350 g) all-purpose
    flour, plus extra for flouring
12 tablespoons (6 oz/175 g) butter, diced
1 egg, beaten
2 tablespoons sugar
⅔ cup (5 oz/150 g) Greek yogurt, mixed
    until smooth and set aside to rest
2 teaspoons (¼ oz/7 g) active dry yeast
Zest of 1 orange

For the filling:

¼ cup (2½ oz/75 g) plum jam
Few squares of Turkish delight, diced

To decorate:

Generous ½ cup (2½ oz/75 g)
    confectioners' sugar

To make the dough, combine the flour and butter in a food processor and pulse 8 times. Add the rest of the dough ingredients and mix on low speed until the dough comes together. Transfer to a bowl, cover, and leave in a warm place for 30 minutes.

Preheat the oven to 350°F (180°C) and line a baking sheet with parchment paper. Flour a work surface and roll the dough out until ¼ inch (5 mm) thick. Place an upturned 12 inch (30 cm) round plate onto the dough and cut around it, reserving the trimmings. Cut the dough circle into quarters, then cut each quarter into two triangles.

Take a little of the jam or 1 dice of Turkish delight, and place it at the wider end of one of the dough triangles. Roll towards the narrow end of the triangle and place onto the baking sheet—it should look like a croissant. Repeat with the remaining dough triangles. Combine the dough trimmings together, roll again, and repeat to use all of the dough.

Bake for 12 minutes or until they begin to change color, and roll in confectioners' sugar while still warm. Make a cup of tea or coffee and treat yourself to two, one of each filling.

Cremă caramel de dovleac cu nucă şi stafide

Pumpkin crème caramel with walnuts and raisins

Here I am turning a beloved Romanian pumpkin filling into a delicate, bitter-sweet crème caramel, served with raisins soaked in orange liqueur. The liqueur is optional, and you can definitely use orange juice alone. My mom used to make crème caramel very often, especially during the summer, when it was too hot to eat doughy desserts.

To make the raisins, heat the orange juice and raisins in a pan over medium heat and simmer for 8 minutes. Set aside to infuse before adding the liqueur.

Preheat the oven to 400°F (200°C). Roast the pumpkin or squash for 20 minutes, then set aside until cool enough to handle. Pulse in a food processor until smooth.

Reduce the oven temperature to 325°F (160°C) and prepare 6 ramekins. To make the caramel, melt the sugar in a pan over medium heat until dark. Immediately pour the caramel into the ramekins and set aside to cool.

To make the pumpkin crème, beat the eggs, egg yolk, and sugar until pale, then add the rum and pumpkin purée. Bring the milk to a boil in a pan over medium heat, whisking continuously, then pour into the egg mixture. Pass the mixture through a fine sieve then pour into the ramekins.

Place the ramekins into a roasting pan and transfer to the oven, then pour cold water into the pan up to a quarter of the ramekins' height. Bake for 40 minutes, then remove the ramekins from the pan and leave to cool. Refrigerate overnight.

When you are ready to serve, run a sharp knife around the inside edges of the ramekins and turn out onto serving plates. Add the walnuts and spoon over the infused raisins.

Serves 6

For the infused raisins:
¼ cup (60 ml) orange juice
⅓ cup (2 oz/60 g) raisins
2 tablespoons orange liqueur

For the pumpkin crème:
14 oz (400 g) pumpkin or squash, diced
4 eggs, plus 1 egg yolk
½ cup (3½ oz/100 g) sugar
1 tablespoon rum
1¾ cups (400 ml) milk

For the caramel:
½ cup (3½ oz/100 g) sugar

To serve:
2–3 walnuts, roughly chopped

CHAPTER SIX

Pickles, preserves, compotes, and drinks

There is a tradition in Romania to welcome guests with a little tray of homemade fruit jam, a glass of cold water, and a coffee. When the fruit is ready for harvest, from mid-summer onwards, we turn into a nation of jam and marmalade makers. Later on in the autumn we start pickling green tomatoes and cabbages in brine and peppers in vinegar, as well as making drinks. There are also more elaborate delicacies, such as stuffed peppers or pickled fruits, the latter sometimes with fish.

It is a never-ending process and when I was little, it was a family (and compulsory) effort. My sister and I both had to pitch in and help however we could, very often having to spend the weekends ensuring that rows and rows of jars were prepared and carefully aligned in cupboards for use later in the year.

We didn't have a house with a pantry: in fact our apartment was really small, and these jars were sometimes split between a cupboard in the hallway, the bookcases in the living room, and some wooden shelves on the balcony. But even so, it was delightful and reassuring to know that we had all these delicacies in the house.

Varză murată şi gogonele

Fermented sauerkraut-style cabbage and green tomatoes

This is a famous duo in the Romanian world of pickles. If you only make this recipe, you will be prepared for the winter. We'll use a 3 quart (3 liter) jar here, but back home, the cabbages would be fermented in large 7 gallon (30 liter) barrels kept on the balcony of our apartment. It was always my dad's task to look after them—he was the pickle "affineur." The cabbage was either dry-salted to draw out the liquid from the leaves or brine was added to aid the fermentation. Although generally associated with German cooking, this method was actually spread across Europe by the Tatars in the 13th century with the Mongol invasion. *Gogonele*, the green tomatoes, are traditionally fermented in 2½ gallon (10 liter) jars and if you have a surplus of unripe tomatoes, this could be a good use for them.

Makes 2 x 3 quart (3 liter) jars

For the cabbage leaves:

1 large white cabbage

1 tablespoon dill seeds

1 tablespoon fennel seeds

4–5 juniper berries

1 apple, sliced

3 bay leaves

1 bunch of fresh lovage (optional)

Slices of horseradish root (optional)

For the green tomatoes:

2 lb 4 oz (1 kg) green tomatoes

1 carrot, sliced

1 parsnip, sliced

3–4 garlic cloves, peeled

For the brine:

8½ cups (2 liters) water

¼ cup (3 oz/80 g) salt

Equipment

2 x 3 quart (3 liter) preserving
    jars, sterilized

2 small plates that will fit inside the
    jars or 4 wooden skewers, to keep
    the ingredients submerged

To prepare the cabbage leaves, scoop out and discard as much of the core of the cabbage as possible. Carefully peel the leaves away one by one, taking care not to damage them. Depending on the type of cabbage, you may need to submerge it in hot water in order for the leaves to come away easily. Place the leaves into one sterilized jar, one on top of the other, adding a bit of the other ingredients with each addition. Fill the jar, leaving 4 inches (10 cm) of head space without pressing the leaves down. Set aside.

To prepare the green tomatoes, place the tomatoes in the other sterilized jar, followed by the other ingredients.

To prepare the brine, bring the water and salt to a boil in a pan over high heat, then carefully pour over the cabbage and tomatoes. You may need to make another batch of brine if this is not enough to fill the jars (it will depend on the volume of your ingredients).

Leave the jars uncovered overnight. The following day, place small plates or wooden skewers positioned like a cross inside the jars to keep the cabbages and tomatoes submerged. Seal with the lids and place the jars in a warm place, ideally over 65°F (18°C) and not in direct sunlight. Open the jars every couple of days to let the fermentation gases out. It's not mandatory, but it avoids having to clean up if the liquid leaks out.

Depending on the temperature of the environment you should

have fermented cabbage in about 10 days and tomatoes in about 14 days. Both will look a little wrinkly. If the garlic cloves in the tomato jars turn a bit blue, don't worry. They are perfectly safe to eat: the coloring is just a reaction that some types of garlic have with the brine.

Use the cabbage leaves to make *Sarmale* (see page 88), and the tomatoes sliced and drizzled with olive oil as a side dish. The brine (if clear and not cloudy) can be used as the souring ingredient in *ciorba*, in place of *borş*, in chapter three (see pages 69–85).

Ardei muraţi

Stuffed peppers in vinegar

Why have simple pickled peppers, when you can have this super fancy version? Serve as a side dish, with a generous drizzle of olive oil and a grating of black pepper

Combine the cabbage and carrot in a large bowl. Sprinkle with a pinch of salt and set aside at room temperature for 1 hour to soften slightly.

Meanwhile, carefully remove the stalks and lids of the peppers and discard the seeds—there needs to be enough room to stuff with the cabbage.

Squeeze as much water as you can from the vegetable mixture and use it to stuff the peppers. Place the stuffed peppers side by side in the jar, cut-side up.

Bring all of the ingredients for the preserving vinegar to a boil in a pan, then remove from the heat. Leave to cool for about 5 minutes, then pour over the peppers. Place a small plate or 2 wooden skewers positioned like a cross inside the jar to keep the peppers submerged.

Seal the jar and store in a warm and dark place (the peppers may be discolored by light). They will be ready in 25–30 days.

Makes 1 x ½ gallon (2 liter) jar

¼ white or red cabbage, finely shredded
1 carrot, peeled and grated
Salt
6–8 large peppers, to fit inside the jar

For the preserving vinegar:
2¼ cups (550 ml) water
1 cup (250 ml) vinegar
1 teaspoon salt
2 teaspoons sugar
10 black peppercorns
3 bay leaves

Equipment:
1 x ½ gallon (2 liter) preserving
	jar, sterilized
A small plate that will fit inside the
	jar or 2 wooden skewers, to keep
	the ingredients submerged

Makes 1 x 1 quart (1 liter) jar

For the fruit:
2 bunches of seedless grapes of different
     colors, separated into small clusters
1 small cantaloupe, skin-on and
     sliced into thin wedges
3–4 plums, quartered and pitted

For the preserving vinegar:
1½ cups (350 ml) water
¾ cup (180 ml) vinegar
1 teaspoon salt
1 tablespoon sugar
1 teaspoon cinnamon
3 cloves
1 star anise

Equipment:
1 x 1 quart (1 liter) jar, sterilized
A small plate that will fit inside the
     jar or 2 wooden skewers, to keep
     the ingredients submerged

Fructe murate

Fruit medley: grapes, cantaloupe, and plums

These are the sort of pickles that will intrigue your diners. They go well with fish dishes, but I prefer to serve them at the beginning of a meal, drizzled with a little olive oil. You can add quince, pear, apple, and even watermelon—pretty much any fruit can be pickled.

To prepare the fruit, place the fruits into the jar, alternating the different types. To make the preserving vinegar, place all the ingredients in a pan and bring to a boil then remove from the heat. Leave to cool for 5 minutes, then pour over the fruit. Place a small plate or 2 wooden skewers positioned like a cross inside the jar to keep the fruit submerged. Seal the jar and store in a cool place. You can try them after 15 days.

Tarhon în oțet

Tarragon in salt and vinegar

This is the simplest and prettiest of all the preserves I make. The different shades of green, the textures of the salt, and the ruffled leaves make this a joy to look at. You can use this method to store any green herbs, but bear in mind that they will become very dark in color.

Makes 1 x 6 oz (180 ml) jar

3 bunches of tarragon
¼ cup (2 oz/60 g) rock salt
½ cup (120 ml) white wine vinegar

Equipment:
1 x 6 oz (180 ml) jar, sterilized

Bundle together the tarragon and place it in the bottom of the jar, then sprinkle generously with salt. Press down well, then repeat with another layer, until the jar is full. Add enough vinegar to cover entirely. Seal the jar and store in a dry, cool cupboard for up to a year. Once opened it will keep in the fridge for up to 2 weeks.

Salată de murături asortate

A salad of assorted pickles

Romanians have a lot of affection for vegetables pickled in vinegar, and every household has at least one jar of pickles of some sort in their pantry. Although the vegetables are usually preserved whole, this version can be made in any size jar you have in the house. The result is a beautiful-looking salad that can be served as a side dish, or as a topping for meat or vegetable burgers to add flavor and crunch.

To make the vegetables, put them all in a bowl and sprinkle over the salt, then set aside at room temperature for 1½ hours.

Squeeze the vegetables well to remove any excess water—I do this in batches, taking only a small quantity at a time—and place into a pan over medium heat. Add the vinegar, sugar, bay leaves, and pepper and stir for 2–3 minutes, ensuring the liquid does not boil.

Pour the mixture into sterilized jars, add the herbs, and seal with the lids. It will keep for a couple of months in a cupboard, but store in the fridge once opened and consume within a week.

Makes 2 x 1 pint (500 ml) jars

For the vegetables:
½ cauliflower, separated into small florets
4 green tomatoes, quartered
2 peppers, sliced
2–3 small onions, quartered
1 carrot, peeled and grated
¼ red cabbage, shredded
4–5 garlic cloves, peeled
1 tablespoon salt

For the preserving vinegar:
½ cup (120 ml) white wine vinegar
1 tablespoon sugar
3 bay leaves
1 teaspoon black pepper
1 bunch of parsley
½ bunch of lovage (optional)

Equipment:
2 x 1 pint (500 ml) jars, sterilized

Magiun de prune

Plum jam

This is one of the most loved jams in Romania, and it is made using small plums. The recipe doesn't include sugar, since the jam needs to be tangy and vigorous, and my personal preference is to add a little lavender to make it really special. Spread it on toast or use it to fill crêpes and pastries, tarts, or cakes. It also goes well with sweetened polenta.

Makes 2 x ½ pint (250 g) jars

2 lb 4 oz (1 kg) plums

Scant ½ cup (100 ml) water

Zest and juice of 1 small lemon

2 tablespoons edible lavender (optional)

Equipment:

2 x ½ pint (250 g) jars, sterilized

Wash the fruit well and place into a large pan with the water. Simmer over low heat until soft and the pits separate from the fruit. Set aside until cool enough to handle, then pass through a sieve to remove the pits. (Alternatively, halve the fruit and remove the pits before simmering, in which case you don't need to pass the mixture through a sieve.)

Return the mixture to the pan, add the lemon zest and juice, and lavender (if using), and simmer until reduced by half. The jam needs to be really set to prevent mold from forming. Transfer immediately to sterilized jars, seal, and store in the pantry for up to 4 months.

Dulceață de vişine

Sour cherry preserve

This is a delicacy mainly because the cherry season is so short. We like to use any cherries—sour cherries, white cherries, and bitter cherries, all of which grow happily in Romania and make the most exquisite fruit preserves.

Pit the cherries and remove the stems. This is the only hard work you'll need to do, and I usually gather some friends around to help me with the task. Put the cherries in a large bowl to collect the juices.

Meanwhile, bring the water and sugar to a boil in a pan over medium heat and simmer until the syrup thickens. To test if the syrup is ready, put a drop onto a plate and see if it holds its shape, like a little pearl.

When ready, remove the pan from the heat and add the fruit. Set aside for 30 minutes, then return to medium heat and add the lemon juice. Simmer for 10–15 minutes until reduced by a quarter, skimming off any foam that forms on the surface with a slotted spoon. Add the vanilla extract and mint, if using, and transfer to sterilized jars. Seal the jars and store in the pantry for up to 6 months.

Makes 4 x ½ pint (250 g) jars

2 lb 4 oz (1 kg) cherries (any that
    are available to you)
2 cups (500 ml) water
5 cups (2 lb 4 oz/1 kg) gelling sugar
Juice of 1 lemon
1 tablespoon vanilla extract
Fresh mint (optional)

Equipment:
4 x ½ pint (250 g) jars, sterilized

Dulceață de violete

Violet preserve

This preserve is truly special, made from delicate violets right at the beginning of spring. I wanted to include this recipe because it has the air of old town Bucharest with its sophisticated amalgamation of cultures and delicacies. My grandmother's neighbor, Madame Tudor, was a talented dress maker and she would receive little thank you gifts from her well to do clients. Sometimes they were very special homemade treats, like looking through a window into a world of a by-gone aristocratic era.

Soak the petals in water and set aside. Meanwhile, bring the water and sugar to a boil in a pan over medium heat. Boil until the sugar is completely dissolved. Turn the heat down to low and simmer until thickened. Drop a little of the liquid on a plate and see if the drop holds its shape—if it does, the syrup is ready. Add the lemon juice and the drained violet petals, and simmer for a further 5 minutes. Pour the preserve into the sterilized jar and seal. Once cool, store in the fridge and enjoy little spoonfuls every time you need a precious treat.

Makes 1 x 5 oz (150 g) jar

7 oz (200 g) edible violet petals
¾ cup (180 ml) water
1 cup (7 oz/200 g) sugar
Juice of 1 lemon

Equipment:
1 x 5 oz (150 g) jar, sterilized

Marmeladă de măceşe cu mere pădureţe

Rosehip and crab apple marmalade

This reminds me of foraging with my grandmother, Domnica, on the narrow alleys of our neighborhood. It was an endearing part of old Bucharest, with traditional urban houses and two-story buildings from the 19th century, cobble-stone streets, overflowing fruit orchards, and hanging grape vines. All of this was to be wiped out by the grand building ambitions of Ceausescu, when we lost so much of our beloved city and our connection with the past.

Domnica was my maternal grandmother, and being from Transylvania, this marmalade of rosehips and wild apples was very much part of her seasonal pantry. So here is the recipe in her memory, for all the hours she spent making delicious food for us.

Makes 4 x ½ pint (250 g) jars

3 cups (14 oz/400 g) rosehips
3½ oz (100 g) crab apples
1¼ cup (9 oz/250 g) preserving sugar
Generous ¼ cup (3½ oz/100 g) honey
Juice of 1 lemon

Equipment:
4 x ½ pint (250 g) jars, sterilized

Wash the rosehips and crab apples and place in a large pan. Cover with water, and simmer over medium heat until soft enough to be crushed into a paste, then set aside. When cool enough to handle, transfer to a food processor together with the simmering water and pulse to a paste-like consistency.

Pass the paste through a fine sieve or a mouli grater to remove the seeds. This is a labor of love, so listen to your favorite radio show or invite a friend over for a chat while you are doing it.

Return the smooth paste to a clean pan, together with the sugar, honey, and a scant 1 cup (200 ml) water. Bring to a boil, then lower the heat and add the lemon juice. Simmer for 30 minutes, stirring regularly.

If you prefer a soft set marmalade, take the pan off the heat and transfer the mixture to sterilized jars. If you like a firm set, simmer for a further 10 minutes before transferring to sterilized jars. Seal the jars immediately.

Once cool, store in a cool pantry. Unopened, they will keep for 1 year.

Dulceață de gogonele

Green tomato jam

I decided to include this recipe to give a helping hand to all of those gardeners who end up with a lot of unripe tomatoes at the end of the season. Traditionally it is made using green plum tomatoes, blanched, hollowed, stuffed with walnuts then submerged in a hot sugary syrup. I have simplified the recipe to accommodate any kind of tomatoes you may have. It will turn them into a beautiful jam, perfect with yogurt, on toast, with doughnuts, or with cheese.

Wash and halve the tomatoes, and set aside. Bring the water and sugar to a boil in a large pan over high heat, ensuring that all of the sugar is dissolved. Add the tomatoes, lemon juice, and star anise. Turn the heat down to medium and simmer until the tomatoes are soft and mushy. Add the walnuts and vanilla extract and simmer for a further 5–10 minutes—it shouldn't look too set or become dry.

Transfer to sterilized jars and seal with the lids. The jam will keep for 4–6 months. Enjoy with pancakes or cheese.

You can peel the tomatoes before adding them to the syrup. It's more laborious but it will result in a finer jam. To do this, submerge the tomatoes in boiling water for a minute to soften the skins before peeling them away. You may also like to remove the star anise before transferring to the jars.

Makes 4 x ½ pint (250 g) jars

2 lb 4 oz (1 kg) green, unripe tomatoes
1¼ cups (300 ml) water
4½ cups (2 lb/900 g) preserving sugar
Juice of 2 lemons
3–4 star anise
1½ cups (5 oz/150 g) walnuts
1 tablespoon vanilla extract

Equipment:
4 x ½ pint (250 g) jars, sterilized

Compot de gutui

Quince compote

I love quince and it is one of the fruits that I have missed eating since I moved countries. My parents had a quince tree in their garden and it produced the most beautiful fruit ready to harvest at the end of October. Stored on window sills, the fruit imparted a delicate aroma into the air. We didn't need air fresheners or other decorations—and the quince were much prettier. We'd even eat them raw as a snack.

Peel and core the quince, then cut into thick slices. Place into a bowl, cover with water, add the lemon juice, and set aside.

Pour 8½ cups (2 liters) water into a large pan. Add the sugar and honey and bring to a boil over high heat. Add the slices of quince, in batches if you don't have space to add all at once. Turn the heat down and simmer for 5 minutes, then remove and divide the quince between the jars. Add a cinnamon stick to each jar then our over the syrup and seal.

Put a dish towel in the bottom of a large heavy-based pan. Place the jars in the pan and fill with water—so the jars are fully submerged. Bring to a simmer, trying to keep the temperature below 194°F (90°C). Simmer for 20 minutes, then leave to cool in the water, overnight if possible.

Store the jars in a cool, dark pantry, or in the fridge. Unopened, they will keep for 6 months—enough to get you through the winter. Serve with rice pudding or sponge cakes, using the syrup as a drizzle.

Makes 4 x ½ pint (250 g) jars

4 lb 8 oz (2 kg) quince
Juice of 1 lemon
1¼ cup (9 oz/250 g) sugar
Generous ¼ cup (3½ oz/100 g) honey
4 small cinnamon sticks

Equipment:
4 x ½ pint (250 g) jars, sterilized

Nuci confiate

Green walnuts preserve

Makes 4 x ½ pint (250 g) jars

Juice of 3 large lemons
2 lb 4 oz (1 kg) green
    walnuts (25–30
    pieces)
4¼ cups (1 lb 14 oz/850 g)
    preserving sugar
Generous ¼ cup (3½ oz/
    100 g) honey
4 cloves
2 star anise

Equipment:
4 x ½ pint (250 g)
    jars, sterilized

Look out for green walnuts in early summer, before they form their woody shell. We had our own from the garden, and mom and grandma used to make this exquisite preserve—a sweet, nutty delicacy. It is an effort of love but totally worth it. We would serve it on little saucers, accompanied by a glass of cold water.

Fill a large bowl with cold water and the juice of 2 lemons. This next part will stain your hands, so be sure to wear rubber gloves. Peel the walnuts and pierce all over using the tip of a knife. (Reserve the peels to make Walnut Liqueur, see below.) Immediately place the peeled walnuts into the bowl of water—make sure the water covers them completely. Place an upturned plate on top of the walnuts to ensure they stay completely submerged. Refrigerate overnight.

The next day, bring 1¾ cups (400 ml) water along with the sugar and honey to a boil in a large pan over medium heat and simmer for 30 minutes. Rinse the walnuts and add to the sugar syrup together with the juice of the remaining lemon and the spices. Turn the heat to low and cook for 20 minutes until the syrup thickens. Keep an eye on the pan to make sure the syrup doesn't become too dark.

Cover with a damp dish towel and leave to cool for 15 minutes. Transfer to sterilized, fairly hot jars, seal, and leave to set overnight.

Lichior de nuci verzi

Walnut liqueur

Makes 8½ cups (2 liters)

Green walnut peels (see
    above)
4–5 apricot kernels,
    crushed (optional)
4 cups (1 liter) vodka
1½ cups (10½ oz/300 g)
    sugar
2 tablespoons honey
Zest of 2 lemons
4–5 cloves

Equipment:
1 x ½ gallon (2 liter) jar
1 x ½ gallon (2 liter)
    glass bottle

Place the peels and apricot kernels (if using) into the jar and pour over the vodka. Seal the jar and leave in a warm place for around 3 months.

Strain the infusion through a cheesecloth. Add the remaining ingredients and mix well. Return to the jar and seal. Return the jar to a warm place for another 6 weeks, shaking it from time to time. Strain the liqueur again and bottle it. It is now ready to serve.

If it is too strong, make a simple syrup with a little sugar and some water and add it to the bottle—but it's really a sacrilege. To make the color darker, caramelize 2 tablespoons sugar and add 1–2 tablespoons of water, then mix it with the liqueur.

Vişinată

Cherry liqueur

Crafted drinks are a staple of any Romanian household, and every year we make our own țuică and vişinată. Țuică is a plum or greengage brandy, served in shots as an aperitif to prepare you for the meal to come. Vişinată is a liqueur made from sour cherries, a little tangy, and exactly what is needed after one of our robust desserts. My dad would add crushed cherry pits to his vişinată to achieve a bitter-sweet almond undertone. I've adapted this recipe slightly to include a tangy element, in case you can't find sour cherries.

Makes 4 cups (1 liter)

1 lb 12 oz (800 g) cherries or
    sour cherries, unpitted
1¾ cup (7 oz/200 g) red or black currants
1½ cups (10½ oz/300 g) sugar
Scant ½ cup (100 ml) white rum
2 cups (500 ml) vodka
½ teaspoon almond extract

Equipment:
1 x ½ gallon (2 liter) jar
1 x 1 quart (1 liter) bottle

Put the cherries, red or black currants, and sugar into the jar and mix well. Cover with a cheesecloth and leave on the kitchen counter, or in a warm place, to begin the fermentation process. Shake the jar every day for 3–4 days. Towards the end there should be quite a lot of juice in the jar, and the sugar should have dissolved.

Add the rum, vodka, and almond extract. Seal the jar and store in the pantry or cupboard for one month, then strain into the bottle. Don't discard the rum-soaked cherries: remove the pits and use the cherries to decorate cakes, chocolate mousses, or wrap them in marzipan and coat them in dark chocolate for delicious candies.

Cafea

Coffee

We have a strong coffee culture in Romania and visitors are often blown away by the number of coffee houses there are in our towns. We take a lot of pride in using special coffee blends, or in returning to the good old habit of drinking Turkish coffee from pure Arabica coffee beans.

    The coffee house tradition is deeply ingrained in our city life. For hundreds of years, coffee houses played an undeniable role in harboring the debates of intellectuals, nourishing the talent of artists, and being the background of political satire. There was a break of around 25 years when they stopped being so lively, but now they are back, unchanged and as artistic as ever. Coffee is still served with slices of cake or tortes, enticing pastry delicacies, cookies, or baklavas.

Cafea la ibric

Turkish coffee

This is the traditional Romanian way to make coffee, in an *ibric*, served black in small cups, with a little teaspoon of sugar. Even the chicory and chickpea coffees rationed during communist times were prepared in the same way.

    It should be brewed slowly, lifting and lowering the *ibric* closer or further away from the heat. This will make the crema on top swell and foam, like a cloud, changing into shapes resembling animals or objects. We always wait for a few minutes before drinking it, while the coffee grounds settle at the bottom of the cup. After drinking, some people like to turn the cup upside down on its saucer to interpret the patterns made by the coffee drying on the inner sides of the cup. It's quite fun.

Serves 2

1 cup (250 ml) water

2 teaspoons sugar (optional)

¼ cup (1 oz/30 g) Turkish Arabica ground coffee or other good ground coffee

Bring the water and sugar, if using, to a boil in a Turkish coffee pot or a small pan, adding more sugar if you like your coffee sweet. Remove from the heat and stir in the ground coffee. Return to low heat, slowly lifting away from the heat when the foam swells, then lowering again. Repeat twice more.

    Skim the froth—the crema—forming on the surface and divide between two coffee cups then pour in the coffee. Wait for the grounds to settle at the bottom of the cups before drinking. Enjoy.

Café Frappé

Ice cream latte

Serves 2

1 heaped tablespoon
    instant coffee
4 teaspoons sugar
Scant 1 cup
    (200 ml) cold milk
2 scoops chocolate
    ice cream

To decorate:
Scant ½ cup (100 ml)
    heavy whipping
    cream, whipped with
    1 teaspoon
    vanilla extract

This is a mesmerizing summer drink combining coffee and ice cream in a delicious way. To me, it will always be associated with spending my summers with my friends at the Black Sea, as an "independent" teenager allowed to travel without my parents. You would have found me eating éclairs on the patios of summer gardens, *terase,* overlooking the beach, and drinking this tall, chocolate concoction.

Put all the ingredients in a blender and blend until smooth and a little frothy. Pour immediately into two tall glasses, add a couple of spoonfuls of the vanilla whipped cream, and slide in a straw. Some people like to use less milk and add cola instead; others like to add a little coffee liqueur or sprinkle cocoa powder on top.

Șodou cu cafea

Bunica Maria's anti-flu rum coffee

Serves 4

2 eggs yolks
3 tablespoons sugar
1 teaspoon honey
1½ tablespoons
    instant coffee
Scant 1 cup (200 ml) milk
2 teaspoons vanilla extract
1 tablespoon rum

My dad's mom, Bunica Maria, had a few homemade methods for curing a cold. Apart from giving us large cups of thin, sweet polenta with milk, or, when we were old enough to take it, a small glass of mulled plum brandy with a good pinch of black pepper, she had this coffee trick. The coffee had to be strong, basically working like a super-powered headache pill, while the rum pulled all the evil viruses out of us, warming us from head to toe.

Beat the egg yolks with the sugar and honey in a heatproof bowl until pale. Add the instant coffee and combine well. Heat the milk in a small pan then slowly pour it over the egg mixture. Keep whisking, then return the mixture to the pan and set over low heat and simmer for 5–6 minutes until thickened slightly. Remove from the heat, add the vanilla extract and rum, and serve in small cups.

Şerbet de cafea

Coffee sherbet

Not to be confused with the frozen sorbet, this recipe is a version of the West Asian and Indian sweet drink *sharbat*. Alongside fruit preserves and jams, *Şerbets* were the testing stone for any respectable and skillful cook, mainly because of the way they needed to judge when the sugar syrup was ready. The hardened sherbet was usually served in a teaspoon placed directly into a glass of cold water. A guest would have a little of the sweet confection, then drink some of the water and place the spoon back in the glass. The sherbet would eventually dissolve, turning the water into a sweet drink.

Put the sugar and water into a pan and gently warm it over low heat, stirring occasionally, until the sugar is dissolved. Increase the heat to medium-high and boil the syrup for 8–10 minutes, brushing down the sides of the pan to prevent the sugar from crystallizing. Drizzle a bit of the syrup onto a plate and if the drops hold their shape, it's ready. Remove from the heat.

Meanwhile, combine the instant coffee with 2 tablespoons warm water in a small bowl until well blended. Add the coffee mixture and lemon juice to the sugar syrup and stir well.

Cover the pan with a wet dish towel and leave to cool for about 15 minutes, or until the bottom of the pan is just warm. Using an electric whisk, start whisking until the mixture thickens. Quickly pour into the sterilized jar and leave to set. It will become hard in a few hours. Aside from using it to create a drink, you can warm it and combine it with a little butter to create a glaze for cakes and cookies.

Makes 1 x 10½ oz (300 g) jar

1¼ cup (9 oz/250 g) sugar
½ cup (120 ml) water
½ cup (1 oz/30 g) instant coffee
Juice of 1 lemon

Equipment:
1 x 10½ oz (300 g) jar, sterilized

Basic recipes

Afumături

Hot smoking

For hot-smoking prunes: Remove the rack from the roasting pan and line the pan with 2–3 layers of aluminum foil. Scatter the wood chips or tea leaves into the pan along with the herbs, then place the rack on top.

Place the prunes onto the rack. If the prunes are small, put parchment paper on the rack first to prevent them from falling through. Make sure to pierce the paper evenly all over, so the smoke can get through to the fruit.

Cover everything, pan and all, with more aluminum foil. Place the pan onto the stove top, across 2 burners, on the lowest heat. Smoke for 40–60 minutes, moving the pan around every so often to expose it to the heat evenly. Set aside to cool.

Heavy-duty roasting
pan with a rack
2 tablespoons smoked
wood chips or the
contents of 2 Lapsang
Souchong tea bags
1 bunch of fresh thyme
or rosemary

For hot-smoking sausages: Follow the same method as for the prunes above, placing the sausages directly onto the rack and covering everything tightly with foil.

Smoke for 30 minutes, then open the foil and turn the sausages. Replace the foil and continue to smoke for a further 20 minutes.

Transfer the sausages to a frying pan over medium heat and cook for 5–8 minutes or until cooked through.

Mămăligă

A side dish of creamy polenta

Bring the milk and water to a boil in a pan over high heat. Reduce the heat to medium and stir in the polenta. Cook for a further 10 minutes, stirring continuously, adding more hot water if necessary until the mixture has the consistency of a thick, firm porridge. Season with salt and pepper, add the butter, and mix well until melted. Serve as a side dish.

Serves 4

Scant 1 cup (200 ml) milk
1¼ cups (300 ml) water
1 cup (5 oz/150 g) coarse polenta
4 tablespoons (2 oz/60 g) butter
Salt and freshly ground black pepper

Mujdei

Romanian garlic vinaigrette

Peel the garlic and crush in a pestle and mortar. Add the oil and a pinch of salt and grind to a paste. Add the water, vinegar, and a little more salt if needed. Stir well and serve as a drizzle on meat or vegetables. This vinaigrette has a strong flavor, with a hotness similar to chili peppers.

Makes ¾ cup (180 ml)

5 garlic cloves
2 tablespoons olive oil or rapeseed oil
Scant ½ cup (100 ml) water
1 teaspoon white wine vinegar
Salt

Mujdei cu roşii

Romanian garlic sauce

Briefly blister the chili in a hot pan and remove the stalk. Pulse in a food processor with all the remaining ingredients and a pinch of salt. Add more vinegar if it's not tangy enough.

Makes ¾ cup (180 ml)

1 green chili pepper
5 garlic cloves, peeled
4–5 cherry tomatoes
1 tablespoon white wine vinegar
3 tablespoons olive oil or rapeseed oil
Salt

Brânză de casă

Homemade ricotta

My grandmother Domnica used to make this cheese all the time. She didn't like to buy it from the shop, because she wanted us to have the freshest cheese possible. In the summer, she would leave the milk to curdle naturally at room temperature, but in colder months she used vinegar. You can also use lemon juice, but we didn't have lemons or citrus fruit in those days.

Makes about 2 cups (10½ oz/300 g)

For ricotta used in doughs:
12½ cups (3 liters) whole milk
¼ cup (60 ml) apple cider vinegar

For ricotta used in fillings:
8½ cups (2 liters) whole milk
2½ cups (600 ml) heavy cream
¼ cup (60 ml) apple cider vinegar

Bring the milk (and cream, if using) almost to a boil in a pot over medium heat. If you have a thermometer, it should be at 198–203°F (92–95°C). Remove from the heat and pour in the vinegar, stirring once or twice. Leave to cool while the cheese curds form.

Cover a bowl with a cheesecloth and very carefully pour in the cooled milk. The curds will be left in the cloth. Lift the cloth and tie the top with a string. Tie it to the handle of one of your kitchen cabinets and place a bowl under the cloth. Leave to drip overnight.

The following day the ricotta will be ready to use in pies and pastries or to eat on toast with fruit.

Înghețată cu cidru

Cider ice cream

Whip the cream to stiff peaks, then fold in the condensed milk and liqueur. Transfer to a plastic container and freeze for at least 2 hours.

Makes 1½ cups (350 ml)

1 cup (250 ml) heavy cream
⅓ cup (80 ml) condensed milk
¼ cup (60 ml) cider liqueur

Frișcă cu vanilie

Brandy Chantilly Cream

Whip the cream with the sugar to soft peaks, then add the vanilla extract and brandy. Leave in the fridge until needed.

Makes 1½ cups (350 ml)

Scant 1 cup (200 ml) heavy
  whipping cream
Scant ½ cup (2 oz/60 g)
  confectioners' sugar
2 teaspoons vanilla extract
¼ cup (60 ml) brandy or Calvados

Seasons and superstitions in Romanian cuisine

Romanian cuisine is highly seasonal. In the summer we cook in the Turkish-Greek style, and in the winter we turn to Slavic and Germanic recipes. These styles come together with specific ingredients and cooking methods. Summers are for grilling meat, fish, and vegetables over open fires and enjoying the outdoors, while winters are for braising cabbages, slow-cooking hearty stews with potatoes and beans, and baking rich *plăcinte* (cakes).

I don't think you can truly experience Romanian cooking unless you are enjoying traditional home-cooked meals. In restaurants serving Romanian food, the chefs will have their own family recipes that they bring to the table. Our traditional food is personal.

Romanian culinary traditions are about celebrating life—marriages, births, agricultural calendar events, and also superstitions and religious beliefs. If you spill salt, you need to drop some water on it to avoid having a fight with someone. We make a cross in the air three times above a loaf of bread before slicing it, as a priest would do in church to bless it. We believe that if we eat the bread crust, we'll be beloved by our mother-in-law forever(!).

Spring traditions

Spring in Romania is a time of festivities relating to the agricultural calendar, to love, or to the religious traditions of Easter.

Măștile is one of the last pre-Christian festivities in Europe. People dress up in colorful costumes, wear impressive masks, and dance on village and town streets in order to scare away the evil spirits of the winter.

Mucenici is celebrated on March 9th and remembers the 40 saints who were tortured by the Romans and lost their lives for their Christian beliefs. Traditionally Romanians drink 40 shots of alcohol, which fortunately is not obligatory, and cook a vanilla and walnut soup with little pieces of dough shaped like the number eight—symbolizing the human form of the martyrs themselves.

Dragobetele is the Romanian Valentine's Day held on February 24th. As with so many of our celebrations, bread is an important element. Small round breads called *colaci* are braided or decorated to symbolize renewal, love, and togetherness, with the braids resembling a hug.

Paştele, or Easter, is the most important religious celebration in our Orthodox calendar, perhaps more important than Christmas. Romanians gather at churches at midnight on Easter Eve (Saturday night) in impressive numbers, and there's a wonderful atmosphere full of excitement, gratitude, and hope, as well as lots of food. Our Easter eggs are not made of chocolate; they are hard-boiled eggs, painted in different colors, that we love to exchange following a little egg-cracking battle.

Summer celebrations

Romanian summers are extremely hot, almost unbearably so, especially in the south and the cities, where stores stay open sometimes until after midnight to allow people to do their daily shopping in less scorching heat.

In the countryside, summer is the time to start using outdoor kitchens, and a time for *hramuri*—communal celebrations of different saints. The whole village gathers around sharing food and reinforcing their bond and support for each other. Traditionally the dishes would be laid on the ground, on immaculate white tablecloths, following the tradition of eating "on the green grass."

A dessert called *colivă* is served at many religious festivities (including funerals). Made with creamed cracked wheat or pearl barley, large quantities of chopped walnuts, honey, and a dash of rum, its wonderful flavors and textures melt in the mouth.

Summer is also the time when acacia and linden flower honey is harvested, and we like to have a little teaspoon of honey on an empty stomach every morning for good health.

Preserving the autumn harvest

Autumn is a very busy time of year in Romanian kitchens. Vegetables are bottled and pickled, fruits are turned into delicious jams and compotes, grilled vegetables are made into a dip called *Zacuscă* (see page 20), plums and greengages are fermented to make brandy, and tomatoes are cooked down to make tomato passata (purée).

Garlic is heavily associated with St. Andrew's Day, Romania's patron saint, celebrated on November 30th. It's believed that wolves can speak on this night and will come out of the woods to attack farm animals, so we make sure that they are all locked away in their stables. This is also the night of marriage predictions. Young, unmarried women bake a salty loaf of bread and eat some before bedtime, hoping that their future husband will appear in their dreams bringing water to quench their thirst.

A winter's tale

Romanian winters are dominated by preparations for Christmas and the tradition of slaughtering a pig. In the past, this was very important for our survival between December and May. The meat and charcuterie products made from it would have fed a family of four for more than six months, so it was an occasion for celebration.

I remember traveling to get the pig with excitement. We used to drive for 5 to 6 hours from Bucharest to Alba-Iulia in Transylvania, where my uncle lived and reared a black-breed pig for us. In two days, everything was prepared from nose to tail, packed, and ready to be taken home.

It was a communal activity, with neighbors pitching in to help. The slaughter had to happen when the weather was cold, dry, and windy to allow some of the charcuterie to air-dry. My uncle also liked to cold smoke meat. He used his own secret wood mix, and we would leave a quarter of the sausages and lard with him for a few months to be cured and smoked. The rest of the sausages would have been taken home to the apartment to be air dried on the balcony—they were a spectacular sight hanging over the washing lines.

Women were usually the ones who prepared all the charcuterie. My mom, sister, and aunts would decide which meat went into different products, then chop it together with fat and offal to go into spicy paprika sausages, rich *leber* (liver-based sausage), intricate *tobă* (head cheese), and dark *sângerete* (blood sausage). The fatback would be used for *Slănină* (see page 23), while the rest of the fat would be rendered and used as lard in cooking and baking. There was a little feast at the end of the first day called *pomana porcului*, which included a pan-fried diced pork dish made to celebrate the pig's life and to give everyone the opportunity to take a moment and be thankful for this loss of life.

It was during this feast that I first understood that in order to eat, we had to sacrifice the life of our farm animals. These pigs (and my uncle's sheep and cattle) all had names, they were treated and cared for incredibly well, and nothing went to waste. Offal, tails, ears, and trotters were all used and consumed in one way or another. It wasn't just because of the rich flavors they imparted to dishes, but for nourishment and sustainability for both my uncle's farm and us.

Romania's culinary heritage

Over the course of many centuries Romania has been colonized by the Roman, Byzantine, Ottoman, and Austro-Hungarian empires and, ultimately, Russia. This has had a massive influence on our history and culture, and the spirit of Romanian cooking really does encompass Europe's varied cuisines.

The Dacians and the Celts

It's hard to pinpoint exactly which passing or settled tribe had the most influence on Romania's staple foods. The Dacian tribes are very likely to have had contact and cultural exchanges with the Celts. Known for being pig herders, the Celts worshipped the spirit of the oak tree and loved chestnuts. Pigs and chestnuts are very much present in Romanian food even today, and the oak has played a role in many events throughout our history.

Wheat, grape vines, and honey could have been introduced by the Greeks, who had settlements along the Black Sea long before the Roman conquest. The grape vine is believed to have originated in the Southern Caucasus, somewhere between Armenia, Turkey, and Iran. This is close to the Black Sea, and many foods could have taken a direct route from Tomis (today's Constanța, Romania's port-city) to reach Europe by sea. It is believed that one time all of the country's vineyards were destroyed in order to keep the Dacian warriors sober.

The Romans

The wealth and vast territories of the Dacian tribes caught the eye of the ever-expanding Roman Empire, and after a series of unsuccessful attempts to conquer it, they made this territory a colony in 105 BC. This meant that people and foodstuffs were coming to Romania from all over the Roman Empire, and with them came *pulsum*—a soup of boiled grains, which is an ancestor of polenta. The Romans also facilitated the introduction of fruit trees such as apricot, peach, and pear; walnut trees; peas and fava beans; pearl barley and millet, from which the Romanian word for polenta, *mămăligă*, originates; and herbs, notably dill, parsley, and lovage.

Later, the invasion of the Mongol Empire can be credited with the introduction of butter-making and sauerkraut, although preserving in brine is thought to be a Chinese invention.

Garlic was brought from Central Asia and was particularly loved throughout the Byzantine empire.

The Ottoman Empire

When the Ottomans introduced maize and polenta, the new grain was initially not taxed by the local rulers, and so became very popular in peasant cooking (not to mention that you get a better yield from a crop of maize than one of wheat). They also brought potatoes, tomatoes, watermelons, eggplants, and vanilla, together with new ways of cooking.

Romanians learned the skills of pastry-making and the layering of fine pastry sheets, as well as how to roll it, stuff it, and soak it in sugar syrup. *Sărmăluțe* (see page 132) and *Sarmale* (see page 88) became popular, made using not only the staple fermented cabbage leaves but also any other leaves that were growing on the land, including grape and linden tree leaves. Rice started to be used in different dishes, and rice paddies were cultivated along the Danube river in southern Romania to feed a growing Ottoman Empire.

The Greeks, Slavs, and Hungarians

The Ottomans made money by selling princely titles in Wallachia and Moldova to rich Greek families established in Phanar, one of the historic quarters of Istanbul. Romanian cuisine became directly influenced by how much the Phanariots enjoyed eating, and they introduced French methods of cooking, already held in high regard throughout the rest of Europe.

Slavic influences brought our beloved *borș* (see page 70) to Romanian cuisine, while Transylvania, which sits in the center, north, and west of the country, was heavily influenced by Austria and Hungary—potatoes, dumplings, strudel, and *tocană* (rich stews) all became popular.

Trade and migration

This amalgamation of ingredients and cooking techniques were based not only on political governance and occupation, but also trade and migration. Jewish cuisine had a role to play, as it had across all of Central Europe during the mass migration of Jewish people, and may be the origin of our beloved chicken soup with dumplings or *pastramă*.

Romany communities, known as *țigani*, came with their own set of crafts, and when they first arrived from north-west India they were kept as slaves by the ruling classes and monks. It is believed that the tradition for cooking meat over open fires was a custom borrowed from them, but the Ottoman soldiers were known for the same thing too. Oppressed by society wherever they went, Romany people were forced to give up their nomadic culture and settle by the communist regime.

Traditional crafts were lost when the Romany people had to find jobs in agriculture and settle on the outskirts of cities and towns—this didn't help their integration into Romanian society. After the fall of communism when they were once again permitted to move from town to town, they were the first to look for a better life abroad.

Bucharest, or Little Paris

The old town of Bucharest is a charming amalgamation of architectural styles. The old cobblestone streets once belonged to different trade guilds with shops at the ground floor and accommodation above. Lipscani street was for those who came from Leipzig with merchandise from Western Europe. Another street was dedicated to saddle makers, one to glass makers, and others to goldsmiths and fur traders.

Later on, the grand boulevards of the 19th century, our French-inspired Arc de Triomphe, the decorative houses and imposing official buildings in the style of Napoleon the Third's Paris brought Bucharest the endearing nickname of "Little Paris." It was a cosmopolitan city buzzing with merchants, automobiles, horse-pulled carts, gypsies selling flowers, bourgeoisie out for a walk, politicians, artists, and writers. Two different centuries and two different cultures were happily living side by side and enjoying that peak time after WWI, a time which sadly didn't last when things took a turn for the worst.

The loss of artisan skills

Communism had a huge impact on Romanian history and culture. The making of artisan products such as cheese, charcuterie, and wine was discouraged, to say the least, and almost vanished. Communism wiped out communities. Whole villages were demolished in order to make room for blocks of apartments, in an attempt to quickly modernize a population that simply wasn't ready. The traditional peasant way of living suddenly moved to an "apartment environment" where people kept doing what they knew best, even growing vegetables and rearing chickens, only now on their balconies.

The regime was on a mission to homogenize traditions. Inevitably cooking, and especially regional cooking, suffered, and we ended up with one cookbook that everybody had to follow even if the basic ingredients were rationed or completely unavailable. Luckily (if you can call it that) there was a black market for recipes passed down by word of mouth or written down on napkins or on loose pieces of paper. My mom kept them in an old chocolate box and we enjoyed making them whenever we could.

Romania's cultural values

Throughout Romania there is a new wave of rediscovering and returning to our traditional values and artisan crafts. In recent years, UNESCO has listed quite a few of our unique contributions to the European heritage. Some of them are regions, sites, or buildings; others are skills, dances, or songs.

The regions

The fascinating ecosystem that is the Danube Delta is unique in Europe for its diverse biosphere and is home to a record number of bird, plant, and fish species. It is part of the territory of an old Neolithic culture called *Hamangia*, where later on the Persians, Greeks, and the Genovese built settlements and diversified their trade. It is a stunningly wild and fascinating region from where Romanians used to export caviar to cities like Budapest and Vienna. Perhaps less glamorous but still important, the Black Sea fish Pontic shad, or *Scrumbia de Dunăre Afumată*, has gained PGI (Protected Geographical Indication) status.

The Carpathia Mountains dominate the landscape in Romania, with more than half of their surface being in our country. Their beech forests are considered to be primeval and untouched by human intervention. They have UNESCO status for being part of just a few similar forests in Europe, populated with brown bears, wolves, chamois, and lynx. Also listed is The Hațeg National Park, for its fossils of a dwarf species of dinosaur that used to live in this part of Europe.

Ibănești cheese is the first Romanian cheese with protected designation of origin for its high levels of calcium and magnesium content, and for being preserved in salted spring water unique to this Carpathian region.

The sites

Sites such as the ancient capital of our Dacian ancestors Sarmisegetuza, and the Saxon towns of Transylvania are also listed by UNESCO. The Saxon communities have a long history in Transylvania, being sent there by the Austrian and Magyar kings to form a bulwark against the infidel, to build fortified villages and churches, and to organize the area economically. They have created a network of beautiful towns such as Brașov, Sibiu, Sighișoara, and more than 250 villages. One of our most loved charcuterie products originating from this region is *Salam de Sibiu*.

The buildings

Two types of Romanian churches are on the UNESCO list—the wooden churches of Maramureş and the painted monasteries in Bucovina. The former are recognized by their slim clock towers and double roofs, representing an intriguing cross between the religious Orthodox architectural style and the Gothic style. The latter are famous across the world for their richly-colored frescoes of Suceviţa and Voroneţ. They made writer Sir Sacheverell Sitwell fall completely in love with them when he visited in 1938.

The crafts

Last but not least, traditional styles of music, pottery, and embroidery have been granted UNESCO status. *Doina* is a style of song about the feeling of loss and longing for love, one's family home, or happiness. The Horezu pottery and the rugs of Oltenia are still made today following techniques and patterns used hundreds of years ago. Henri Matisse painted *La blouse roumaine*, featuring our traditional blouse made of cotton and embroidered by hand with intricate patterns. The work became an icon for traditional eastern European art throughout the world.

Picture credits

p.1 © Dunca Daniel Mihai/Alamy; p.2-3 © Danm/Getty; p.8-9 © Dinosmichail/Alamy; p.14 above left and right, 46 above, 184 above right © Irina Georgescu; p.14 below © Coldsnowstorm/Getty; p.46 below right © Andrea Ricordi/Getty; p.56-57 © Dace Znotina/Alamy; p.68 above © Bob Gibbons/Alamy, below © EyeEm/Alamy; p.86 above right © Xalanx/Getty; p.86 below © Vlad Sargu/Unsplash; p.94-95 © Serban Draghici/Alamy; p.104 © Petr Svarc/Alamy; p.128-9 © Alexionutcoman/Getty; p.138-39 © Posnov/Getty; p.144 below © Graham Prentice/Alamy; p.164 © Mel Longhurst/VW Pics/Universal Images Group via Getty Images; p.178-79 © Cta88/Getty; p.184 above left © Mihnea Turcu, below © Adrian Petrisor / EyeEm/Getty; p.224 © Florin Brezeanu/Alamy

Index

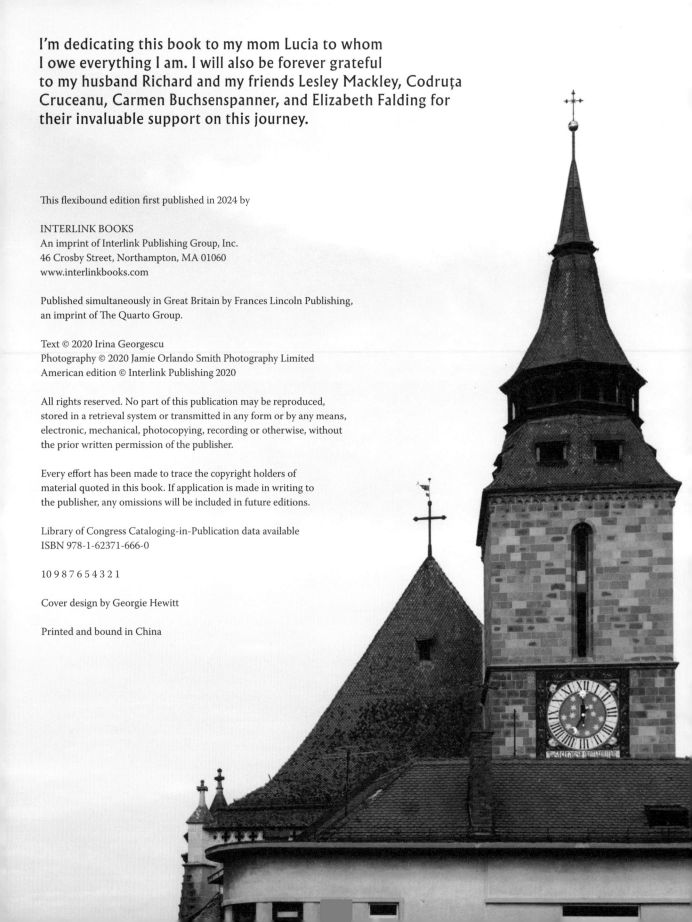

I'm dedicating this book to my mom Lucia to whom
I owe everything I am. I will also be forever grateful
to my husband Richard and my friends Lesley Mackley, Codruța
Cruceanu, Carmen Buchsenspanner, and Elizabeth Falding for
their invaluable support on this journey.

This flexibound edition first published in 2024 by

INTERLINK BOOKS
An imprint of Interlink Publishing Group, Inc.
46 Crosby Street, Northampton, MA 01060
www.interlinkbooks.com

Published simultaneously in Great Britain by Frances Lincoln Publishing,
an imprint of The Quarto Group.

Text © 2020 Irina Georgescu
Photography © 2020 Jamie Orlando Smith Photography Limited
American edition © Interlink Publishing 2020

Library of Congress Cataloging-in-Publication data available
ISBN 978-1-62371-666-0

10 9 8 7 6 5 4 3 2 1

Cover design by Georgie Hewitt

Printed and bound in China